FULL COLOR LIFE

MIA WALSHAW

Evatopia Press

Evatopia Press, a division of Evatopia, Inc.

Copyright © 2016 by Mia Walshaw

ISBN: 978-1-63099-101-2

To Simon…who brings full color to my life and makes every day as magical as those when rainbows appear.

Preface

_____

The Rainbow Analogy

When sunlight hits Earth, the light appears white. In actuality, white light is made up of a spectrum of colors. If that beam of sunlight happens to hit raindrops on its way down, we will see the colors that comprise it. The result: a rainbow.

The light changes speed both when it enters the raindrop, and again as it leaves. With the change in speed, its path bends and refraction occurs. As light rays are refracted, various wavelengths are effected. What occurs next is increased separation of the component colors of white light, known as dispersion.

Here is the more simplified explanation of how rainbows occur. Some light is *reflected* when it hits a water droplet. The rest of the light is *refracted*. The white light splits into color and the phenomenon is known as *dispersion*.

That beam of light is highly complex, just like us. Only at certain angles can a rainbow be seen. I equate this to our own creativity. The power to be creative is within all of us. Yet, just like that beam of light that must hit the raindrop at precisely the right angle for a rainbow to come into view, our mind, body, and spirit must be primed in order for creativity to not just be released, but to flourish. To illustrate this point, this book is divided into three parts: Reflection (Full Color Mindset), Refraction (Full Color Health), and Dispersion (Full Color Spirit).

In Reflection, I talk about our mindset and how to nurture **self-belief** about your creative abilities. In part two, Refraction, I discuss how our physical health affects the creative process. Here, we focus on **discipline**, not just in the sense of working diligently on your creative craft, but by also maintaining optimum physical health, which is proven to positively affect our creative process. Finally, part three of this book is Dispersion, a discussion on **perseverance** and how to nurture one's spiritual self so that you can weather the storm and channel sunlight to create your own personal rainbow.

Introduction

Unleash Your Inner Creative

I've worked with creative people my entire adult life. Most are writers, but I've also promoted musicians, artists, clothing designers, boutique owners, jewelry makers, soap creators, chocolatiers, and sculptors. Phew! Basically, I'm proud to say that I've become a magnet for creative people. Perhaps because the feeling is completely mutual; I love creatives and couldn't imagine not working with people whose minds are in perpetual motion.

One thing that happens time and time again is that one of these artisans will admit that they wish they could... and here's where I fill in the blank with whatever creative endeavor is being discussed at the time.

I've met book bloggers who dream of writing a novel, not just blogging about other people's work. I know food bloggers who dream of moving past their time in front of the computer and into the kitchen where they can start a culinary business.

There's a certain appeal to being creative and it extends beyond artists to people who work in fields that are not considered traditionally creative. My accountant admitted to me that he has an idea for a spy thriller novel. When my mechanic found out what I did for a living, he told me wistfully that he's always wanted to write a book.

Being creative is something that garners mixed reactions in people. Many say they love creative activities but are quick to show modesty — almost apologetically saying they aren't very good at it. Others say they wish they led a more creative life, but fear or again modesty, keeps them from pursuing it.

One blogger friend told me, "I could never write a book." Although just prior to stating that fact, she said how she wished she could. So what's holding her back from at least trying?

As children, we are encouraged to try new things and we readily listen. The assumption is that it's okay if you're not very good, you just have to give it your best shot. We see this in terms of sports and even trying new foods. Yet, somewhere into our adulthood, this attitude shifts. Isn't it strange that fear grips us more as adults than it does as children? Or is it that we don't have someone standing over us, encouraging that one spoonful of okra into our mouth? (Honestly, is there anyone who likes it?) Still, we're told to "just try it" as if at age eight we truly have a choice.

We may have developed our fair share of insecurities as adults, but we also have a strong sense of what we're willing to try. Imagine life like the Thanksgiving table. There are a myriad of choices. As you move around the buffet table or pass serving plates from one relative's hands to the next, you decide which dish will find its way to your plate.

Creativity can be a similarly conscious choice. You don't have to wistfully consider a parallel life and wish yours could include a creative element. You can add this to your life. The result will be an improvement in every aspect of your life from your mental well-being to your physical health, and even your spiritual nature.

You will become more satisfied with your life, which will lead to better relationships with your family and friends, even your co-workers. There aren't any get rich quick schemes, but if you want to make a living with a creative endeavor, I promise it won't happen if you don't try it.

This book assumes one thing: If you're reading it, you have the desire to be creative. I'll go one step further and assume that you would like creativity to play a major role in your life. You're probably feeling mixed emotions right about now. A big part of you wants to jump in without fear, but there may also be a tinge of self-doubt holding you back. Commitments such as a spouse, children, and our jobs take up the majority of our time. You may wonder if there's even enough time to add one more thing.

But what if that "one more thing" is the creative endeavor that will give you so much pleasure, make you feel whole, and leave you energized so that everything and everyone around you benefits as a result?

At its core, *Full Color Life* means to live a creative and balanced life, acknowledging that we all have existing responsibilities. You can learn to incorporate creativity into your existing lifestyle with glorious results that will improve your daily lives and future.

The world is made up of procrastinators. I can be guilty of this as well. I can even argue that my preferred procrastination activity is cleaning. Weird, I know. But it's a useful habit. If I'm not writing at least my counters smell lemony fresh. I even remember a few years back there was a best-selling book called "Sink Reflections" that endorsed and supported my cleaning habit. The author, Marla Cilley, said to start each day by cleaning your sink to get a sense of accomplishment, a fresh slate so to speak, to start your day and ensuing productivity.

It's a great start, but it's not going to result in a novel being written. Cleaning your sink is fine. Procrastinating by cleaning everything around you will not result in a book. A creative endeavor is a bit like a rainbow. People are in awe of them, but they only materialize if the circumstances are right and for writers that means you're writing. Simple as that.

People will ask an artist what he does and he'll reply, "I paint pictures." They'll say, "Oh, that sounds like fun. I wish I could make that my job." But to say this is to belittle how hard it is, how disciplined the creative must be to go into the studio each day. If it were easy, everyone would be making a living at it.

There's your dose of tough love mixed with a reality check. Now here's the magically appearing rainbow. The process can be learned. You can train yourself to be disciplined. And best yet, practicing a creative endeavor will improve your life.

This book isn't just for writers and artists, dancers and chefs, artisans and musicians. It's for anyone who enjoys the creative process and wants to incorporate more of that into their lives. It's for people who feel their days fold into their nights and then wake up and repeat the cycle without reward. This is your guide for how to live a creative life, and by doing so, improve your mental, physical, and spiritual health.

Read on. Enjoy the journey. Live life creatively.

Part I

Reflection - Full Color Mindset

"Anyone can train to be a gladiator. What marks you out is having the mindset of a champion." — Manu Bennett

The Creative Appeal

The creative's life is not always easy. This is especially true if you measure your success solely on monetary earnings. But it's important to take a step back and consider what else you value. If I were to answer this I would list: family, friends, good health, and time — the one gift that nobody can buy and nobody can give you. There's one thing that I feel enhances each one of my core values and that's my creative endeavors, whether they are writing my own work, editing others' work, or being physically creative in a dance or yoga studio, which helps me stay mentally focused and physically healthy, both of which fuel my spiritual creativity.

So, why did you decide to pursue your creative endeavor? Here are some other common reasons: creative control, independence at work, and the ability to make changes at a moment's notice. In many ways, this last reason encompasses the ones before it. If you work for yourself, there are fewer surprises. You know if a big order is coming or if a client is unhappy. Both good news and bad gives you independence. If something isn't working, you have time to spot it and change your course. That is creative independence and you can't get that while working for someone else.

Remember why you toyed with the idea of a creative career in the first place. You dreamed of a creative life with independence, financial security and being able to call the shots. But it's not always like that, is it? There will be moments of self-doubt when you launch your book or product line and wonder what the public response will be. Times when inspiration flees and you question if you're cut out for a creative life. Periods when mounting bills make it seem like the daily grind of your current job will not only be your present but your future as well.

It's the tough times that test a creative individual. When scenarios like those mentioned above crawl their way into your psyche that's when you must have self-belief…a Full Color Mindset.

There are plenty of books on the market that promise riches if you follow their course of action. I don't believe in false promises. When it comes to living your creative dreams, you have to take responsibility for your role in your future. Here are a few tough truths:

> *I can't make you rich.*
> *I can't make you famous.*
> *I can't make you more satisfied in your life.*

What I can do…I can inspire you and show you how others before you have taken action and achieved their success.

It takes hard work. As stated earlier, this book focuses on three areas of your life: your mind, body, and spirit. Those areas correspond to three core values you must hold: **self-belief, discipline, and perseverance**. Each one of these elements is necessary for you to find success personally, in your immediate relationships and in your business relationships.

We view some cultural and celebrity icons as having achieved overnight success, but on closer inspection, we begin to realize that many of these creatives worked tirelessly for years. None were actually picked from obscurity as the media may have claimed…although that makes a darn good story.

Scattered throughout this book you'll find the success stories of Will Ferrell, E.L. James, Justin Bieber, and other creatives who are equally inspiring in their own fields. Read them as a means of inspiration with the knowledge that everyone who has obtained success has shared the core values listed above.

The Rainbow Mindset

B efore we can live a full color life where creativity fuels our soul, we must focus our thoughts, practice mindfulness, and be present. Some people may be familiar with these concepts as "yoga terminology," but it applies to everyone who wants to improve their lives and relationships. This isn't just the relationship you have with colleagues, family and friends, but also the one you have with yourself and how you view yourself.

The Rainbow Mindset is how we fit into the bigger picture. Consider the way a photographer views his subject. Some will take a photo with the subject being crisply defined while others may employ different creative strategies to blur the edges and redefine the image. One is more structured; the other more relaxed.

This is not an argument for one lifestyle being better than another. Rather, it's a methodology for determining how creativity can best fit into your personal style and life responsibilities. By looking inward, we can develop a productive, creative practice that fits into our lifestyle without sacrificing current responsibilities.

But first, let's establish an argument for why this is

important. You're plugging along quite well, thank you. Why change? You're comfortable in your own skin. You know what to expect from the day. Change is something a chameleon does so why adopt the habit of a lizard, a species that will shed its own tail the minute it feels threatened?

Why? Because actually that's quite a smart characteristic this plucky little creature possesses. Can you imagine being able to have a do-over every time we get ourselves into a bit of trouble? Now's your chance.

YOUR FULL COLOR LIFE GOALS

Let's establish our Full Color Life goals. Here are some obvious choices pertaining to the artist in all of us:

> * *I want to do something creative, not just the nine-to-five drudgery.*
> * *I want to make a living from my creative endeavor.*
> * *I want to improve my outlook at work while pursuing this endeavor.*
> * *I want to find more time to pursue this endeavor without sacrificing my relationships.*

You may have some of your own to add to this list. Go ahead and write them down. Make yourself accountable to your own goals.

Here's a hard question for you. (Remember, I don't believe in false promises and I never said this process was an easy fix, a get rich quick scheme or a change your life overnight sort of deal.) So here it goes…

Have you ever taken stock of what aspect of your life is working and what isn't? Sometimes it's easier and more comfortable not to consider these facts. But go on, be hard on yourself. When you launch a creative endeavor that is burning inside of you and begging to be freed, your critics are likely to be hard on you. Take this opportunity to critique yourself first. It's with a good measure of self-reflection that we can later move into self-belief. Your strong sense of self-belief is what's going to help you weather the reviews and critiques.

> **Sometimes, by looking inward we discover external processes that are needed to foster our own success.**

Of course, you'll also need to become your own expert. In working with writers, I've read my share of scripts. It shouldn't come as a surprise that not all of them are worthy of being produced. That in itself isn't what is most disappointing to me when I'm searching through the slush pile. It's the egotistical letters that often accompany the script that make me cringe. I often wonder if the screenwriters have taken the time for self-reflection by asking themselves if they're worked their hardest at creating a sales-worthy script. Have they taken time to educate themselves on the screenwriting craft by reading award-winning scripts or even popular movie scripts?

Writers need to be readers. If you're a novelist, you should be reading novels, particularly those of the same genre you write. If you're a screenwriter, you should be reading movie scripts along with watching them. Some writers fear that the work they read will influence their writing. Influence and plagiarism are two vastly different ideas. Being influenced by another writer's work is positive. We admire someone's style and strive for their level of expertise. This isn't copying. This isn't laziness. On the contrary, it takes effort to learn from someone and then emulate their skills. You wouldn't think there was anything wrong with a tennis player watching videos of Serena Williams and then returning to the court striving to deliver a serve the way she does.

In order to be the best, you have to know how your product or skill set stacks up against the competition. Failures are inevitable, but remember…without them there is no room for learning, which leads to improvement.

Every failure should be looked upon as equal parts education and experience.

I knew a top ranking sales executive for a Fortune 500 company that would speak to crowds about the secret to his sales success. He told the group before him that every time he tried for a sale and was rejected, he got a little happier. Crazy? I don't think so. It takes someone of strong convictions with a deep sense of self-belief to react the way he did. He learned that it took him on average ten sales calls before he came to the one that said yes. He knew that one would happen. It just didn't happen overnight. Furthermore, he learned the method for weathering the tough times and cultivating mental clarity.

You can do the same. A Rainbow Mindset means you have an innate sense of optimism, but you are willing to reflect on patterns that have either led to success or had less than stellar results. Sometimes when we aim to develop this mindset, we might find that pieces of the puzzle are missing. Perhaps that optimism doesn't shine as brightly as it should. What if we only see the failures and not our successes?

It's okay. This book will teach you self-belief. Similarly, you will learn reinvention. You will read how others have achieved their ideal creative life. And as you work toward this, you will find that each day brings you closer to your Full Color Life.

3

Embrace Change

W hy is it that when there's a rainbow people will stop and stare? They'll even go so far to point it out and make sure that anyone within arms's distance sees it too. Why? Because quite simply, it's magical. Colors floating in the sky on a crest that has been romanticized about in fairy-tales and movies.

People with a rainbow mindset encompass similar aspects of the environmental science phenomena. They are reflective. Their bodies are maintained to top physical performance. They maintain a spiritual element in their lives. They are a balance of mind, body and spirit.

Rainbows may originate from white light, but as in life, this phenomenon emphasizes the fact that nothing is black and white. Life is a multitude of colors depending on your mood and what's currently influencing your life. Think of your brain in the same respect as a rainbow or prism. Light comes in, which we might refer to as a lightbulb of ideas. We process these ideas and then the prism of our mind reflects on them and disperses them out where we act upon them.

We are just as complex as the prism of light. In order to

be successful in terms of finances, career, health and our relationships, one can't simply consider "seven habits." We must develop practices that work in concert with one another so that being effective in one area naturally trickles into others. To be successful, one must focus on oneself as a whole. The mind, body and spirit working together to create your "inner rainbow" — the most vibrant 'you' that can exist.

With creativity in all areas, we reinvent ourselves and in doing so, find more satisfaction and balance in our lives.

With consistency in your pursuit of success and balance along the way, with a healthy dose of realism, you can achieve the goals you previously outlined for yourself. Let's start with a common goal that many people have…to increase their wealth.

The goal of this book is to help you achieve goals through creativity while improving your life balance. This means that some goals need to take priority over others. So assuming you want to increase wealth, you must first take stock of how doing so will affect the other areas of your life. Putting in too much time with your career or a new creative endeavor may end up taking time away from your family or personal health.

It's important to recognize that some goals may seem unobtainable at first. Rainbows don't appear in the sky simply because you wish for them. Everything must align correctly. The light must bend at just the right manner when it enters as well as when it leaves for raindrops to create the dispersion of colors. The same is true for our goals.

Achieving new found wealth may initially seem blurry or out of focus. Improving one's personal healthy may seem a bit more obtainable. Choosing to concentrate on one over the other does not mean you are ignoring one. It means you are learning to redirect your efforts where they are most needed. This is focus and it makes a difference with your future success.

One can't keep doing the same thing over and over hoping for a new result. This applies to writers who aren't willing to try new marketing tactics, actors who try out for the same types of roles, musicians who pursue the same audience repeatedly. Improvement and change are necessary in order to stay relevant.

Remember the goals you outlined from the previous chapter? Whether they are the ones that I listed or additional ones that you added to the list, write them down and paste them somewhere visible so you can refer back to them often.

Psychology Today posed questions to their readers to determine life satisfaction. In our pursuit of our goals and a Full Color Mindset, determine if the questions below are applicable to these goals.

* Do you try new experiences?
* Do you try your hardest in everything you do?
* Do you enjoy spending time with other people?
* In your everyday interactions, do you approach people with a desire to get along?
* Are you easily upset by different kinds of problems?

If you answered "no" to the majority of these questions, perhaps it shines a light on some areas of your life that could benefit from change. You may not know how to make the change, but the first step is to commit to doing so.

There is only one corner of the universe

**you can be certain of improving, and
that's your own self. — Aldous Huxley**

Similarly, the first scientific step in the creation of a
rainbow is reflection. Self-reflection is imperative to estab-
lishing your own creative mindset. Let's breakdown the
word Reflect for how it can affect and influence our lives in
respect to the concepts discussed in this chapter.

R - Radiate positivity because it's contagious.

E - Ego has its place, but keep it in check. Self-belief is
necessary for the creative entrepreneur, but eliminate the
part of ego that keeps you from seeing your foibles and
mistakes. The negative aspects of ego keep us from developing and growing. Instead, ensure that you always strive for
improvement.

F - Fear is damaging. Throw it out for it will keep you
from living your dreams.

L - Learn everyday. Ideas are everywhere and the best
way to stay current with your own craft is to learn from
others and the world around us. Take time to read and learn
as it will keep you relevant.

E - Experiment and accept that not every idea will be a
good one. Give yourself the gift of accepting that mistakes
happen.

C - Care for others while pursuing your dreams; a pay-
it-forward attitude will serve you well.

T - Transparency in your life is about keeping it real.
Take stock of your situation on a regular basis. Be prepared
to change things up without hesitancy or fear in order to
move forward.

WELCOMING CHANGE

· · ·

NOT ONLY DO YOU HAVE TO EMBRACE CHANGE, YOU HAVE to welcome it. I'm not talking a polite invitation, but an open your door, come on in sort of welcome. Change will keep you fresh and accountable. It will make you relatable to new audiences, particularly younger audiences.

Even companies that have been around since the 1950s like Hanes panty hose strive to stay relevant with new products and current campaigns. A social networking site known as Emode was plugging along in business before it hired a San Francisco naming firm, Igor International, to come up with something that would be more attractive and intuitive to its target audience. It was decided that the new name would be Tickle, and immediately, the company saw a 30% increase in traffic to their site, doubling the value of their business.

Like these companies that take the time to launch new products or look inward to determine if their name accurately reflects their corporate personality, you need to be willing to embrace change and reinvent yourself. You're probably reading this book because on some level you have already made the determination that some sort of change in your life is needed. Now it's time to change the way you think about change.

> *Try this mantra on for size…*
> *Change leads to growth.*
> *Growth equates to new experiences.*
> *Experience is passed onto others.*
> *By helping myself grow, I strive to help others.*

This is a pay-it-forward attitude that starts with your own personal goals and a pledge to never become complacent. In terms of our mind, the first part of our Full Color goals means we must constantly strive to learn new skills.

People in their forties, fifties and beyond may struggle

with the rapid changes in technology. If you fall into this category, take comfort in knowing that the internet has all of the answers to your questions and no question is too simple for your computer. It won't judge you for Googling a question. Need someone to actually show you how to do something rather than just write about it? Try typing your question into YouTube. I taught myself html coding via YouTube and I'm pretty proud of my websites. I know a book cover artist who learned Photoshop from YouTube. You can do it. You need to believe it.

For those who are in their twenties and thirties, you may already experience a relatively high level of success in terms of marketing. Those under the age of twenty have a pretty impressive following on all mediums. However, keep in mind that the steps you took to grow your business or exposure that initially yielded great results, may not remain relevant tomorrow. You must reinvent yourself. Always.

4

The Creative Journey

As a writer, I ask myself a series of questions to help me focus the premise of my story before I start any new project. I might ruminate over the locale where I want the story set or the profession I want my protagonist to lead. Even if you are creative in a different medium such as cooking or art, you still need to begin by asking yourself the questions that will steer you toward what you want to achieve.

A chef could ask what spices he wants in a dish, or what region or style of cooking he desires. A jewelry artisan might ask what stone she wants as the centerpiece or if the piece is avant garde or romantic.

> ***As a creative, part of your job is deciding what emotion you hope to invoke in your customer.***

Keep this in mind when you start each creative journey. I recommend coming up with at least ten questions to help you decide what experience you hope to deliver.

. . .

HERE ARE MY TEN QUESTIONS FOR STARTING THE WRITING process:

1. Whose story is it?
2. Where are they coming from both mentally and physically?
3. Where do they wish they were? (Maybe they like their place and in that case the story will focus on jarring them out of a comfortable existence.)
4. Who will help them?
5. Who will hinder them?
6. What new skills will they develop or what do they learn?
7. What loss will they experience?
8. What is their greatest joy or biggest disappointment?
9. How do they change their world or how do they adjust to changes around them?
10. How are they different from when they started?

All of the answers to these questions may not be included in your book, but knowing the answers will certainly help you create richer, more well-defined characters who engage in original dialogue while they navigate the intricate plot turns that you set them on.

For writers, these questions tend to be introspective as you think about the characters in your book. You'll ask yourself what they want. If you work in a different creative field, the process takes on a slightly different course. You'll want to think of your customer's journey.

FOR CHEFS, ARTISANS, OR PERFORMERS, TRY THESE questions on for size:

1. What mood do you want to create?
2. Do you want your customer's experience to change and evolve or remain steady?
3. What emotion will be fulfilled in your customer as they embark on this experience?
4. What does your customer want and how can you deliver it?

The questions you ask yourself are designed to get your creativity flowing and more importantly, focused. Anyone who has ever had a tennis lesson or tried to hit a baseball has been told, "Keep your eye on the ball." The same lesson applies to business. You must think of your customer and what you want to achieve in order to build a business that has a loyal following.

By getting into your customer's mindset, you establish your own.

5

Leaving Comfort Behind

66 "I know too many people who are stuck in their jobs but have the passion to do something greater. Try things out -- even if it's on the side at first. That's how you grow." Lyndsay Cruz, Oxfam Advisor

W hat's stopping you from jumping into your own creative pool? Fear of failure? Embarrassed to admit that you don't like your current path? Or is it that you dwell over time, feeling there either isn't enough of it or you feel too many other people have gotten a head start and you can't catch up?

It's not that these aren't valid concerns, but they are also empty fears. They are the type of concern that will one day lead to regret, which to me is far worse than fear or embarrassment. We can overcome fear by trying and experiencing. We can get over embarrassment by getting over ourselves. But regret is a negative emotion that stays with you.

There was a time when I felt the regret of not trying and for years, I lived with this feeling while I ignored my passion.

I dreamed of being a writer. I had even written a book, printed it out in preparation to let people read it, and then I decided to keep it in my drawer — where I deemed it safe.

There are a number of reasons why I finally took the plunge and hit that publish button. I bore a deep sense that I needed to do this to be fulfilled, which is what I now encourage others to do. Ironically, the regret that I speak of with such distaste entered my mind. Yet it was different. I knew in my heart, that if I didn't write and publish, I would one day regret it. Admittedly, I also felt that if others could do it, I could too. And who knows…maybe I would be good. I knew that I wouldn't learn the answer unless I went for it.

So, I did it. I published. And nobody saw the book.

That wasn't the truth you were expecting. But it is the truth and it was a let-down. I hadn't considered what lay ahead of me. I was so focused on overcoming a fear of failure in the form of bad reviews that I hadn't even considered the more realistic situation. That is, the internet is a very big place and how is someone supposed to find my little book if I were too scared to talk it up?

It was time to overcome my next fear and this one went against everything I had been taught as a child. Specifically, to be modest and humble. Although I was encouraged to feel proud over my achievements, conceit was not something to admire. This foundation made it difficult for me to later self-promote.

Breaking out of my comfort zone both in terms of publishing and later promoting was necessary to move forward with my goals. Comfort is paramount in my book in terms of a good night's sleep. You'll never see me camping (or even "glamping") because to me that is not a vacation option, but I throw comfort out the window in terms of my personal development and you should too.

Consider the scenarios if you choose to remain where it's safe versus venturing out of that zone.

. . .

IF YOU'RE IN THE COMFORT ZONE, YOU INNATELY BELIEVE:

- This is what you deserve.
- It can't get any better.
- People who achieve more than you do are smarter, more clever, more deserving than you.

ALTERNATIVELY, IF YOU DARE RISK LEAVING COMFORT behind, you agree with these statements:

- I'm willing to learn new skills in order to improve myself.
- I believe that my creative passion is of value and worth pursuing.
- I strive to live a life where I can achieve success through my creativity.

I chose to go with the leaving comfort behind options and have never looked back. I can honestly say it was the best choice of my professional life. After the initial release of my book and hearing crickets following its launch, I picked myself up and began to tell people. I blogged. I shared my interests. I researched innovative marketing strategies. I engaged with other authors. In short, I dared put myself out there both in terms of helping myself and others like me.

The results: book sales, positive reviews and then more book sales. Even better, it made me realize that this creative career choice was viable and important.

Now it's your turn. Do any of my previous concerns sound familiar or perhaps one of these?

- *I don't have time.*
- *I'm not sure my idea will work.*
- *I have too much on my plate to take on something else, even though I wish I could do it.*

No excuses. It's time to get out of the negative mindset and into the creative mindset.

6

Reinvent Yourself

When we reinvent ourselves by conceptualizing what we hope to be and combine it with what we know we are capable of being, that's when we are most open to our creative gifts.

Sometimes reinventing ourselves isn't a matter of change. It's simply adapting to a new mindset. In the previous chapter, I talked about the creative mindset. Do you think of yourself as an innately creative person? If so, are you satisfied in your creative journey?

As we explore this, let's first examine what's so special about creativity? In Hollywood, they've even turned the word into a noun -- "creatives." These are the people who are revered and sought out by hundreds of hopefuls every day. They are the ones who write the films and television shows we watch. If you've ever submitted a query to a literary agency, you must think of yourself as a creative. Even if you work in an outside field that is not typically known for being creative, such as accounting, medicine, engineering, or a corporate office, sending out your work is the first step of your creative journey. You're basically telling the person on the other side of your query letter that you've done something you are proud of. Own it. Call yourself a creative.

Without creativity in our lives, our actions become repetitive and mundane. Creativity is what makes us explore, try, and dare. You might say to yourself, "But I'm not an adventurous dare-devil type of person." I wouldn't classify myself as that either, but I'm certainly creative and I bet that you have that in you as well. Anyone who has ever thought of a solution to a problem is thinking creatively. In her book, "InGenius: A Crash Course on Creativity," author Tina Seelig, who is also director of Stanford's Technology Ventures Program, explains that creative thinking opens up a pathway for invention and discovery.

Everything we use in everyday life — food processors to eyeglasses, jet engines to lasers — whether it's a high-tech invention or simply an object to make our daily lives more manageable, came to fruition when a creative individual was faced with a problem. The problem was met with an opportunity and the result was creative innovation.

E.L. JAMES: A LESSON IN REINVENTION
From Fan Fiction to Publishing Success

BEFORE THE WORLD KNEW HER AS E.L. JAMES, THE author of the "Fifty Shades" trilogy was Erika Mitchell, an English writer struggling like many before her to find a publisher. What Erika did differently from the masses was not to let "no" define her. True, her success story may have had a different ending had she not pursued her dreams in the internet age, but it wasn't just technology that sent her on her path, but also her own ingenuity.

As a former television executive, E.L. James understood

the importance of reinvention and discovery. One can't expect to try something that doesn't work, continue trying it, and suddenly get a different result. So, rather than send out a body of work to agents or publishers and wait the exorbitant amount of time for an answer, often times to have that answer be negative, she tried her hand at fan fiction.

For those who don't know, "Fifty Shades of Grey" began as fan fiction for "Twilight." E.L. James shaped a novel out of her fan fiction stories calling it "Masters of the Universe," and had it appear in installments on several websites. James later compiled the stories onto her own website using her pen name and sold it as an ebook.

The Writers' Coffee Shop, based in Australia, published a print-on-demand version and soon followed up the first installment with Fifty Shades Darker and later, Fifty Shades Freed, until in April 2012, Vintage published a print edition of Fifty Shades of Grey and Universal Pictures and Focus Features secured the movie rights.

The three "Fifty Shades" novels have sold over 100 million copies worldwide, over 35 million copies in the United States and set the record in the United Kingdom as the fastest selling paperback of all time. In 2012, Time magazine named E.L. James one of "The World's 100 Most Influential People." In 2013, James topped the Forbes' list of the highest-earning authors with earnings of $95 million, which included $5 million for the film rights to "Fifty Shades of Grey."

FREE YOUR MIND

LET'S ASSUME YOU'RE PUMPED UP, READY AND WILLING TO be creative, but something still holds you back. Getting past a stumbling block or a creative writer's block can be as simple as just letting go and allowing your brain to move freely into an imaginative zone. How do you do this? Let's first examine what stops our imagination in its tracks.

Brain research conducted by Charles Limb at Johns Hopkins University revealed that our self-monitoring instincts are literally turned off during creative endeavors. Self-monitoring is what makes us not simply blurt out whatever we are thinking or take any physical action that comes to mind. What's curious is that these are characteristics that we are taught at a very young age. It's worth mentioning that we aren't taught to be innately creative, but perhaps we should be.

In order for us to engage our creative instincts, we must in essence turn off the portion of the brain's frontal lobe that is responsible for judgement. This doesn't mean that we'll suddenly run amok. Rather, you are giving yourself permission to relax and allow your mind to speak freely — even if we aren't allowed to whine in public. But this is your creative time. Pursue it freely.

It doesn't matter if you wear another hat. There is no hidden rule that engineers can't also be writers. Has anyone ever said that people who work in insurance can't cook? Of course not. Before John Grisham wrote "A Time to Kill" he spent 60-70 hours a week practicing law at a Southaven, Mississippi law practice. At that time, he called writing "a hobby" and fit in time to work on his first novel before work and during courtroom recesses.

The book was rejected by multiple publishers. Still, Grisham embodied two important characteristics for entrepreneurial success: passion and self-belief. Immediately after completing "A Time to Kill," he started his next novel.

Finally, Wynwood Press purchased "A Time to Kill" and gave it a modest print run. The second book, "The Firm," sparked one of publishing's greatest success stories when film rights were sold to Paramount Pictures for $600,000. Subsequently, Doubleday purchased the book rights from Wynwood Press and the novel spent 47 weeks on the New York Times bestseller list becoming the best-selling novel of 1991.

You're Not Alone

The passage above as well as others that will appear in this book are designed to give you a feeling that you're not alone. Sometimes we view the people on top of their field with a sense of removed wonder. They seem almost untouchable, godlike in their success. We don't often read about their struggles prior to their success.

In our Instagram and Snapchat happy society with every moment of our lives being put on record, many people work especially hard to put their best foot forward. All too often, it leaves the rest of us feeling a bit inadequate. But remember, every one was "just starting out" at one point in their life. Just because they don't reveal their struggles doesn't mean they didn't have their share.

Obstacles — whether internal or external — are present for everyone. Furthermore, just because you jump over one hurdle, doesn't mean there won't be others that follow. The trick is to remember that if you did it once, you can do so again.

I wrote earlier about overcoming my fear of sharing my work. Once I started to successfully get my name out there, I was approached by more writers wanting my help. However, I wasn't in the same situation in terms of life responsibilities that I was following college. I was now married with three children as well as a career. Sounds good, right? Well, if you're in the corporate world, marriage and family can sometimes be seen as a liability. I wasn't sure that clients would be receptive to my circumstances.

I had started my career in entertainment public relations before moving into literary management. I learned that representing companies to the media wasn't that different from representing screenwriters to production companies. But there was one significant difference.

The majority of the development executives I pitched were single and more willing to work well into the evening to prove that nothing would stop their quest to get ahead. I was putting my work day on pause between the hours of 2-5 p.m. to pick up children from school, help with homework and then prepare dinner. I resumed my work afterward, and in essence I probably worked longer hours considering my day didn't end until close to 10 p.m. But I still had to overcome the fact that my "typical" day wasn't the same as the average person in my field.

Clearing Away the Smokescreens

My biggest obstacle to being a working mother was not my three children, not my unconventional schedule, but my own mindset... rather, my insecurities over whether my business could thrive alongside my developing family.

Even though I put in long hours, I still felt the need to put up a smokescreen when inevitably the phone would ring during my personal "do not disturb" hours when the three kids surrounded me.

Then, it was a mad dash to grab the phone and hide in a closet where little voices couldn't be heard. Once, when my daughter was only five, she thought it was a game of hide and seek and to my horror as I spoke to an executive from one of the studios, she did her best "tah-dah" of waving her arms at me in glee that she had discovered my hiding place.

I pleaded with my eyes and shushed her silently with a finger over my lips while pointing to the phone with my other hand. The phone, now cradled between my shoulder and the side of my chin, was giving me a neck ache, but the pain of that moment had to be endured because the reality of admitting that I had children or even worse was working from home, could not get out.

And then I had enough.

I loved being a mother. It wasn't something to be ashamed of and hidden in a closet. In fact, it gave me life perspective that enabled me to offer insight for projects involving marriage, family, togetherness — basically anything that affects the majority of people over 35, and might I add…the book buying audience. Let me tell you, you've never quite felt frustration until a twenty-two-year-old fresh out of college graduate sits in a development meeting to discuss whether a particular book should be adapted to a film and their answer is 'no' because according to them, couples in their forties having sex isn't believable. True story.

It was time for me to embrace myself — my whole self. The business woman. The creative. The mother. The wife. All of my selves make up the whole and that whole has something to offer. And you do too. Your life experiences give you perspective that can be used and capitalized upon.

Most of us have similar goals. We want to feel fulfilled in our career and earn a good living while caring for our family. Some of us have more on our plate than others. Some must care for elderly parents or very young children who take up more time. Some of us are special needs care-givers. But at our core, we share a commonality of wanting to feel a true sense of happiness.

Being a working parent is not a reason to not pursue a business. Similarly, having a job is not a sufficient reason not to pursue a creative endeavor. As we move forward in this book, I'll discuss how we can do both with balance and fulfillment because to not do so, is doing yourself a disservice. Creative endeavors are scientifically proven to be one of the most fulfilling ways to feel good about our lives.

Follow the facts. By doing something good for yourself, you do good for others.

Your Creative Gift

P eople often talk about the tormented artist, but I've never witnessed such a person. When I'm in a room with other writers, I feel at home. The conversation flows freely, if not sometimes like a river with non-stop bends and changes in direction, but that's what makes it so much fun. When I'm with another writer I feel like we 'get' each other. We're cut from the same cloth with the same goals and ideas. We don't just look above and see a cloud, we see the shape of an animal, a smiling face, or even a whole story.

Artists of all sorts whether they are writers, painters, musicians, artisans, chefs, jewelry designers, or clothing designers are all 'creatives'. If you are gifted with ideas and the desire to turn those ideas into something tangible, then you are also a creative.

Those ideas are your creative gift. As we approach or enter adulthood, responsibilities such as mortgage payments and car repairs sometimes interfere with our creative gift. The ideas don't flow the way they did when we were children with wide-eyed optimism. It's true that as adults we have responsibilities, but it doesn't need to banish your youthful joy or the hope you once possessed.

After speaking at a conference, I was approached by a woman who thanked me for my workshop and told me it inspired her. She went on to say that she always dreamed of writing for a living, but "never had the guts" to really make a go of it. When I returned from the conference, I wrote a blog post on margerywalshaw.com called "A Writer Writes!" and made sure to send it to her. This was the response I received back:

> "Your message was one I desperately needed
>   to hear. I'm a stay-at-home mom with
>   three young children. When people ask
>   me what I do, that is what I always tell
>   them. But that isn't what I **want** to tell
>   them.
> What I want to tell them—what I want to
>   shout from the rooftops, in fact—is that
>   I'm a writer. Sure, barely anyone reads
>   what I write; I've never been published,
>   and it probably goes without saying that
>   I've never been paid for a single sentence.
>   In other words, no one really gets
>   anything out of my work, but me.
> But I love it, straight up. So I keep writing,
>   regardless.

Below is the reply I sent. It may have been meant for that one reader, but I think it is just as apropos to anyone reading this book.

> A writer writes! You're not going to be inspired
>   every moment of every day. Similarly,
>   when you are inspired and the writing
>   flows, you may come back to it later and

realize it wasn't very good. You can't expect that every thing to come out of your brain is Pulitzer Prize material. You're human. But that gives you the power of resilience, which means you have to be a grown up.

Get up each day and try. If your story isn't flowing, write about something else, anything else. Make up a fake boyfriend and write a love letter. Describe the beach at sunset. Feeling like something more edge-of-your seat exciting? Write something Stephen King-esque like what you think your neighbor gets up to in that creepy shed of his.

You have to live the life of a writer, which means writing...every day. I promise if you do this, it does get easier.

This brings up the point of what does one do if the ideas simply won't flow? Being creative is more than having a desire for it. It's about learning to tap into a part of your brain that is often undeveloped in adults. Fortunately, it's a skill set that can be learned. Read on...

MALCOLM GLADWELL WROTE ABOUT "THE 10,000 HOUR rule" in his book, "Outliers." In a nutshell, this concept stated that "ten thousand hours is the magic number of greatness." If you can put in 10,000 hours at anything, one will not only become proficient, but great. This applies to writing or painting or dancing. Gladwell's message is that people aren't born geniuses or experts, they get there through effort. I argue that the same goes for ideas. Cultivating ideas is a process that we can practice and as a result, get better.

Whereas Gladwell developed a theory, when applied to brain processes, this has since been proven as scientific fact. Although many people have heard that creative people are "right-brained," science involving studies of the brain are now finding that both sides of our brain work together to become creative. Thus, the creative process combines multiple brain processes.

Our brain hemispheres may have different processing styles, but they are connected. Creative thinking stems from three areas or networks of the brain: attentional control network, imagination network, and attentional flexibility network.

The attentional control network allows us to be "on task" by helping us to pay attention. The imagination network is pretty self-explanatory; it allows us to imagine future scenarios or remember those in the past. This network helps us to create mental images. Finally, the attentional flexibility network monitors what's going on around us as well as within our brain. It's the switch that goes between the imagination network and the attentional control network.

Creativity results when we reduce activation of the attentional control network while increasing activation of the others, the imagination and attentional flexibility networks. Now that you know how these brain centers work, let's break down how you can activate them by viewing creativity and the development of ideas as a process that can be learned and practiced.

WHAT IS AN IDEA?

•   •   •

AN IDEA IS REALLY JUST A NEW FANGLED APPROACH TO AN existing problem or concept. Screenwriters do this all the time and you've probably heard someone pitch a movie by saying it's "Terminator" meets "Alvin and the Chipmunks" — a movie combination you will hopefully never see — but you get the idea. In screenwriting, we're told that there are only seven plots. These are: 1.Overcoming the Monster, 2.Rags to Riches, 3.The Quest, 4.Voyage and Return, 5.Rebirth, 6.Comedy, and 7.Tragedy. Yet, we have thousands of movies produced each year. How is this possible? It's because every idea is really a re-creation of an existing one.

One must be able to see relationships and an interconnectedness of our existing ideas in order to create new ones. So when trying to come up with a new idea, take heart in knowing that the roots of that idea already exist. You just have to retrieve them. The science of creativity says that the best way to do this is to simply relax and trust in yourself.

Consider what you already know and then, experiment in your own mind with seeing things in a new manner. When you trust yourself to come up with an idea, you'll relax into it. People who have never done this are hesitant to believe it's possible, but that is exactly where the trust comes in.

Think of it this way...we often wonder if we can trust someone else. Do we ever ask if we can trust ourselves? This in itself is a new way of thinking. Perhaps, the idea of relaxing and trusting that ideas will come to you is worth taking to heart. I like to think of writers' block or a void in what we consider to be a good idea like a hibernating bear. Eventually, it will wake, and when it does, it's going to stretch, take a look around, and assess its world. It's going to look at things with fresh eyes since the old is sure to have changed during that long sleep.

To learn this skill, you can approach it in two surprisingly different manners. The first is through complete relaxation. Learn to meditate by starting in either a seated or lying down position. Don't put pressure on yourself to relax. That's the last thing you need. Simply focus on your breathing. Train yourself to enjoy this time and set simple goals such as trying to sit still for just two minutes. Ironically, you want to clear your mind. You need to make space for the ideas to enter.

Relax or meditate for a few minutes each day. Do it in the same space, preferably at the same time of day. Make a commitment to doing this just as you make a commitment to work on your creative endeavor each day.

By doing this, you're building trust in your own subconscious. Trust that by letting go, the ideas will enter. However, just because you can trust your subconscious, doesn't mean you can trust your memory. Make sure you write down those ideas that are certain to follow. This brings up the second method for jumpstarting ideas, which is to write down everything that comes to mind.

When you do this, it validates the process of creating in your brain. Ideas breed new ideas. Even better news is that you'll find that the more ideas your brain develops, the better those ideas will become. But this too takes time.

Anne Lamott is a wonderful writer and writing teacher. In her book, "Bird by Bird," she talks about "shitty first drafts." I love this chapter for the very real reason that I'm probably guilty of this every time I write. My first drafts are horrible, but I never start rewriting until I'm finished with that first draft. I don't want to stop the flow of ideas. I have to trust that I'll fix those bad drafts, and I do.

In fact, research conducted at MIT, the University of California Davis, and reported on in an article in *Psychology Today*, all noted that when people record a high volume of ideas, they can't help but have some bad ones, but they are more likely to have good ones. Best-selling author and speaker Seth Godin noted that entrepreneurs and creative people must be willing to produce bad ideas.

By challenging your brain regularly and making it primed to get to work, along with trusting in the process, you ensure that the good ideas will flow when you need them.

AN INTERVIEW WITH MARIA FERRO

Celebrity hairstylist Marie Ferro was the first woman guest to be on Oprah's television show. She counts numerous top Hollywood actresses as her clients and has been written up in *Vanity Fair* magazine for her creative and expert hair fashion advice as well as had her hair makeovers grace countless other magazine covers.

MW: In your line of work, what skill set is most important for your success: being creative or being business minded?

MF: I've been in business for 25 years, but I find that even business must be creative in order to survive and thrive. Creative people will sometimes ignore the business aspects, but one needs to focus on both. Successful creativity is opportunity meets preparation.

MW: Do you find that most people want to be creative?

MF: Most people like the *idea* of being creative or known for something. Creativity isn't a gift. It's hard work and practice. Malcolm Gladwell described it best…you need to put in your 10,000 hours.

MW: Your work is a form of creativity and you provide it to others who are creative…actors and actresses. What characteristics do you possess that you also recognize in your celebrity clients that leads to success?

MF: There are people who have talent, but not perseverance. And, you'll find people with less talent than others, but more perseverance. You need both, but without the perseverance, you won't find success. You also need a strong character and a personality that says you believe in yourself.

MW: Does creativity breed imagination?

MF: I don't think there's anything truly original. Instead, people are inspired by things they see or hear. We are all interconnected by the same information and our brains are wired to connect, but it's what you do with that information that affects your creativity.

8

Facing Fears

"It's so important to understand your strengths
and weaknesses," says Rosie Huntington-
Whiteley, Supermodel and "Mad Max" star.
"For me that means setting goals that are
realistic but still aspirational."

For people who have trouble completing a creative
project I ask, "What are you afraid of?" Here are some
possibilities:

Embarrassment: *People might laugh at your
idea or pursuit.*
Bad Reviews: *You'll never get criticized if you
don't put yourself out there.*
Loss of Focus: *It's better to play it safe and focus
on what you know.*

Let's tackle and subsequently, throw out each one of
these.

37

EMBARRASSMENT:

FIRSTLY, I HIGHLY DOUBT THAT ANYONE WILL LAUGH AT your goal. That's the petty behavior that is saved for teen age angst movies. Let's admit to one truth: laughing at someone's attempts is a pretty unsocial thing to do. If someone laughs at your dreams or attempts, maybe you should reconsider your friends. I know, easier said than done. It's possible that someone who is a permanent fixture in your life is less than supportive, but again, that says more about them than you. You may not be able to walk away from the negativity, but you don't have to let it affect you.

Stay positive and if your existing circle isn't supportive, you can add to your creative community. Find a writer's or reader's group where you can enlist the help of others to read your early drafts. Share success stories as well as failures and learn what others do to bounce back. You're not alone and you'll find if you can lend a sympathetic ear to a writer friend who has had a setback, they'll be there for you if you experience the same.

Another point of view on the subject is to think like a publicist and realize that at least they're talking, whether the chatter is embarrassing or not. Make this your challenge. Make them talk, laugh, and wonder about you. And then promise yourself that you will prove how to be a success.

In an article written by Ilan Mochari, Senior Writer at *Inc. Magazine*, he shares that people can become more comfortable with embarrassment simply by acknowledging that their lives will not be destroyed if their book doesn't sell or they're turned down by a date. Instead of being para- lyzed with the fear of a potential embarrassment, adapt a growth mindset and go for it. Don't let the possibility of feeling embarrassed prevent you from trying.

————

Reviews:

BAD REVIEW BLUES? EVERYONE GETS THEM FROM TIME TO time. Twyla Tharp, an amazingly talented choreographer, who has created more than 130 dances for her own dance company as well as the Joffrey Ballet, The New York City Ballet, Paris Opera Ballet, London's Royal Ballet, and my favorite…American Ballet Theatre, has even experienced a bad review. She told a story in which she got bad reviews at the opening of "Movin' Out," a new show that was inspired by the music of Billy Joel. Most importantly, she did not let bad reviews stop her, nor did she allow them to ruin the rest of the show's run.

She went back to the studio with the intention of making a change that would put the show on a better track. The problem, of course, is that it's not always easy to know what to fix. In this case, she had to determine if the problem lay in the music, the narrative, or visuals. In her own book, "The Creative Habit," she implores creative people to "clean the slate and look at everything fresh." After paying careful attention to the negative reviews (and knowing which ones have something of value to say), she focused on the part of the show that was making people scratch their heads and then applied new choreography to it. The musical went on to earn a Tony Award.

Thanks to the digital age, authors can do the same. If you pay close attention to reviews and make adjustments accordingly, one can upload a new manuscript in less than a minute and Amazon will have the new version online in less than a day. Writers couldn't do that in the days of large print runs. I still believe that it's not the best idea to be laser focused on your reviews, especially if there are outliers — some that are very good and others not so good. The extreme reviews that are positive or negative may have a bias to them. Focus on the majority and if those all consistently have the same complaint or for that matter, the same compliment, try to attack the troublesome aspect and let your strength shine through in future work.

Additionally, in order to get positive reviews for your work, you must obviously have a body of work. It's easy to see the finish line and dash towards it, but I encourage you to enjoy the creative process and see the value that comes when you take your time, plot out a project carefully, and realize its full potential before sending that project into the world only half-baked.

Take these analogies into consideration. The chef must experiment with sauces and spices, cooking methods and combinations of ingredients. The artist will contemplate different color palettes and the composition of the foreground to the background. It's no different for a writer who should experiment with tone and point of view.

None of these creative professionals get it perfect the first time. Creative endeavors are a bit like baking bread from scratch. You combine the ingredients and let it rise. You need time for it to rest before the perfection of the final result can be conceived. Along the way you might experiment by adding in different ingredients to the bread -- cheese or garlic. Or perhaps you add ingredients to the top -- sesame seeds or cinnamon. Every experimentation will yield a different result. Bread can't be rushed and neither can creativity. You just have to put in the time. But, it does get easier as you put in regular time.

Loss of Focus:

As for the last fear that keeps people from trying something new, it's complete fabrication. The very idea that you might not try something new for fear of it keeping you from doing something existing is crazy. Take confidence in your ability to be inspired and your desire to try. It's what dreams are made of. Furthermore, if you aren't pursuing a new venture for fear of losing focus, it probably shows that you aren't that passionate about the new idea in the first place.

The creatives that I know can't help but pursue their craft. It drives them and keeps them going. If you aren't pursuing an endeavor because you want to play it safe with an existing job, I understand that sort of fear. But pursuit of your craft doesn't have to be an all or nothing endeavor. You can play it smart and keep the day job while pursuing your creativeness on the side. In fact, it's this sort of grown-up mindset that will help you achieve your creative goals and potentially make them a full time endeavor.

If you dream of cooking, you taste and smell the possibilities around you. Artisans see materials for use in their product at every turn. Writers hear a song on the radio and an idea for an entire story blossoms in their mind. Each one of these creatives can't help but be creative. It's in their soul, they just have to have a bit of courage to unleash it. Jumping in with both feet is your antidote to fear. More about this below…

What happens when you play it safe?

. . .

AT THE TIME OF THIS WRITING, MY ELDEST SON IS HEADED toward college application time. He's studying for the ACT exam, being active with extracurriculars, taking as many AP classes as he can handle, and learning the nuances of writing a college application essay. To prepare for this last task, we attended an informational lecture about what college admissions officers are likely to be interested in. One quite difficult question in the guise of an easy one, repeatedly came up: *"Who are you?"*

The lecturer explained that this was the question in which teens could tell how their experiences have shaped them as individuals. More specifically, they want to know how failures have formed you as a person or how hardships have made you dig deeper. My husband and I gave each other the uh-oh look and we noted that my son wore the same expression.

"We're too normal," I whispered, although in truth, none of my friends or family would ever describe me with that adjective. What I meant was my son had grown up with two parents who loved him and were still married to each other. He has siblings, two dogs, a home in a suburban neighborhood, plays sports on the weekends, likes pizza, and whenever we can all agree, we sit down for a family movie. Not only is the family too normal, my son hasn't experienced any real failures. This is not what the admissions officer said they look for in a college essay, but it certainly got me thinking.

Was I suddenly regretful that my son had never experienced hardship or a publicly humiliating failure? What about myself? Conversely, I can remember plenty of embarrassing incidents growing up. Similarly, as an adult, I can easily think of a number of times when a business plan didn't go quite as smoothly as I had hoped. One will probably be permanently etched in my memory because it ended up affecting my family.

I was in the midst of negotiating a book-to-film deal between an author and two production companies. The first production company was smaller and although they had experienced their share of success, they were still much less powerful than the second. We needed the second production company to provide the financial muscle and experience to bring this project to a television network. What ensued were meetings that proved to myself, my client and the first production company that I had brought on board, that we were at the mercy of what the second production company wanted. They made it clear that they would call the shots and the rest of us felt the sting of being powerless.

During a family trip to Disneyland, I found myself spending nearly the entire day on the phone, negotiating between the two production companies who seemed intent on fighting each other on every point. Finally, an agreement was made, although it placed the first production company at a disadvantage in terms of their creative control. Still, they agreed to move forward and I was relieved.

At the time, I didn't label the incident a failure, but now looking back, it really was just that. I had failed my family by putting work before our time at Disneyland. I had failed the first production company by not being stronger. I had failed my client by not allowing his vision for the show to be heard. At the risk of sounding as if I'm making excuses, my reasons for all of those mistakes were inexperience.

I stayed on the phone when I should have ignored the calls because I was afraid of losing the deal. I didn't push for the rights of the first production company because frankly, the second company was a very big fish and the rest of us were initially happy to just be invited to swim in their pond. My client agreed that while he hated their vision for his book, we needed to be pragmatic and not take actions that could sully the deal. We both figured that with this big sale, others would follow and we would be in a better position next time with more power to put our foot down to creative changes that weren't to our liking.

We could have been stronger and walked away with our heads held high. But, the deal went through and it's decidedly possible that it wouldn't have if my client had expressed his disappointment to me and if I in turn, played hardball with the development executives.

So we played it safe. Looking back, that is what I feel is the lesson in failure. Yes, a deal was cut and it was a good one. But, at what cost? Certainly creative control and personal satisfaction were sacrificed.

Nobody wants to fail, but if you think of failure as the time that you put yourself out there and then learned from the mistake, I bet you that you'll never make that same mistake twice. Without this "failure" perhaps you haven't moved forward to learn anything. A new endeavor cannot be pursued with passion unless you are willing to try new things, risk failure, and then pick yourself up having learned important lessons that can be applied the next time.

I'm willing to bet that…
most of us learn more from failings than we do in our greatest successes.

9

If Onlys

To be creative is not something that some people have and others don't.

It's not something that is exclusive to writers or artists.

It's not an intangible state that some people never achieve.

To be creative is a choice. And it will dramatically improve your life.

Let me break down the scientific facts about being creative.

CREATIVITY IS A STRESS RELIEVER

CREATIVE EXPRESSION CAN BENEFIT YOUR BRAIN AND mental health to make you a happier, healthier person. In addition to creative writing, activities in the arts such as painting, drawing, and photography have been found to lower your stress levels, leaving one with increased mental clarity.

This is because creating provides a distraction and gives your brain something to focus on outside of our normal daily grind. When we become immersed in a creative endeavor, some people say they are in the "zone." This isn't an accidental phrasing. The same health benefits that meditation provides can be found when you push aside worries to focus on creativity.

CREATIVITY FOR SELF-ESTEEM

REMEMBER WHEN YOU WERE LITTLE AND YOUR MOM would paste your art work on the refrigerator? Writers get this same feeling of accomplishment every time they create a body of work and write those two magical words…The End. Painters can do so by signing their name.

Creating art increases dopamine in the brain, which is known as the "feel good" neurotransmitter. It boosts drive, focus, and concentration as well as stimulates the creation of new neurons and prepares your brain for learning.

Furthermore, the art you create doesn't have to be on the level of Pablo Picasso to register this result. Simply by spending the time doing something creative, you automatically increase dopamine and as a result, ward off depression and protect the brain from aging.

BANISH JUDGEMENT

STILL, PEOPLE HAVE FEARS ABOUT CREATIVITY. Judgement starts to come into play as some wonder, "What if I'm not good enough?" Here's a simple truth that "creatives" already know…to be creative is to live a creative life. The more you practice, the easier your craft comes to you and you will start to incorporate creativity into areas of your life that are not innately creative. The mundane will become less so as you focus on your creative endeavor.

We've discussed pursuing creativity for the sheer enjoyment of it. I've outlined the mental health benefits of being creative, and later in this book we'll learn that creativity also positivity effects physical health. But let's face it, while it's nice to do something for the love of the craft; it's even better to get paid for doing it. With that in mind, one can't give into the high when a bright new idea strikes only to suffer from the low when it gets tough to sell your product or service. Without a distinct sense of self-belief, people suffer from "if onlys".

HERE ARE SOME COMMON "IF ONLYS":

> ** If only I was already famous, then anything I*
> *create would be accepted by my audience of loyal*
> *followers.*
> ** If only I had money, I could manufacture and*
> *distribute my product right now.*
> ** If only I had a team of people working for me I*
> *would be able to fast track my plans.*

If onlys are damaging and I'm telling you to banish them immediately. They don't serve you well because they minimize the truth that every endeavor takes talent, hard work, perseverance, and being able to spot opportunities.

If you happen to have a song playing in the background while reading this, perhaps you don't believe me as there seems to be a wealth of people who seemingly "make it" overnight in the record industry. The same can be said for the film and television industry. But this isn't true. And I'm going to give you the examples to prove it right now.

Shawn Mendes, age 17, used social media to find his audience and became a sensation appearing on Billboard's "21 under 21" hit list for 2015. With his song, "Stitches," Shawn crossed over from being dubbed the "next Justin Bieber" to becoming a bonafide star in his own right. Shawn knew the power of networking and via pop princess Taylor Swift, worked hard until he was catapulted into stardom. But he followed the pay-it-forward caveat to help fellow singer Troye Sivan, just 20 years old, find his place on the same Billboard chart.

Sivan had been uploading YouTube videos since he was twelve-years-old. He didn't truly become known until 2014, which if you do the math means he was uploading videos, networking, and knocking on doors for seven years.

Two examples of young people who with talent, the perseverance to pursue their craft, and the ability to spot opportunities to network, rose to the top. Neither was the overnight sensation story that the public originally believed. It took years of hard work for both of them.

Still, you might be naysaying and continue to believe that money would give you the power to perhaps move to a new town where opportunities are more plentiful. Here's an example from the other side…the story of a man and company with fame, power, money, a strong support team and still, in spite of all the ups, he had to deal with the downside as well. I'm writing about Harvey Weinstein of The Weinstein Company, one of the most well-connected men in Hollywood.

At the time of this writing, it was reported in the *The Hollywood Reporter* that the summer of 2016 wasn't the best of times for The Weinstein Company. Two of its films slated to open in Summer of 2016 were bumped to 2017 raising questions about the company's financial solvency.

His company was also reported to be troubled by executive departures and was cash poor to sustain an upcoming awards campaign. But Weinstein is the epitome of perseverance. His adoption drama known as "Lion," a true story set in India, wasn't getting the talk that Weinstein needed and then, the Toronto International Film Festival made all the difference when he entered the film. Now, not only is The Weinstein Company once again a king in the jungle of Hollywood, "Lion" is generating Oscar buzz.

JUMPSTART CREATIVITY

THE MOST EFFECTIVE WAY TO BANISH "IF-ONLYS" IS TO take actionable steps that will ensure your own success. None of the creatives mentioned above gave up when the going got tough. None rested on their laurels hoping to be discovered. If you want to make it, you have to make it happen.

Sometimes, it's as simple as getting yourself inspired. Keep this list at the ready in case you ever find yourself in the doldrums and need a hand to pull yourself out.

- take a class
- attend a lecture
- meditate
- play
- listen to music
- make your own music
- get outdoors
- cook

- exercise
- read
- draw or paint

These are definitive steps that will allow you to take your creativity into your own hands. People who are go-getters and live for results will relish the idea of doing something today that can jumpstart a creative flow.

But what if, gasp…must I say it? What if…creativity eludes you? You want it desperately, but the ideas just don't come. In Buddhism they say to "relax in the flow of life." This is meant to imply that the answers will come…in their good time.

> "There are only two mistakes one can make along the road to truth; not going all the way, and not starting." Buddha

Can we trust that to be true? In a word, yes. Phrases such as "if-only" and "what-if" have no bearing in our creative lives. We can be as type-A as we want, believing that our internal drive will give way to external results. Trust me, I've had these moments in my life. I fully believed that if I wanted something to happen, it was up to me to make it happen.

And while this book is dedicated to the concept of discovering your creative path and pursuing it with a vengeance, that doesn't mean the time table might some-times frustrate you. The key is to fully accept and believe that by staying on the path, we will achieve our goals.

For most people, this is easier said than done. When our day goes as planned, we feel settled and in control. Conversely, start a day by leaving the house late, driving a bit too fast, getting a traffic ticket, arriving at our destination to find that our purpose has been thwarted, and we will be left feeling frustrated and stressed.

One can't say they won't ever be late and feel nervous at the prospect of what happens as a result. The key to avoid this sort of stressful situation is looking at the bigger picture. It's not a matter of simply setting the alarm an hour earlier each day, although for some that type of time management works. The answer lies in how you accept the unexpected turns your life takes.

A late start doesn't justify speeding down the road. My husband's maternal grandmother wisely said, "Better late in this life, then early in the next."

I take that advice to heart and while I plan accordingly to be on time, living in Los Angeles means dealing with unpredictable and heavy traffic. Sometimes, I have to accept what is out of my control, make the inevitable phone call that I'm going to be late and hope that it doesn't affect the outcome of my meeting.

But if that journey down the road takes longer than I expected, that's when I open my eyes to opportunities that may otherwise go unnoticed. A song on the radio can bring inspiration. A news interview may bring insight.

Letting go of control and worrisome thoughts such as "what-if" doesn't mean giving up our goals, it simply means releasing our internal struggle. Venturing back and forth along the journey can result in interesting scenery to take in along the way. It doesn't mean that we won't eventually bring ourselves back on course.

It doesn't serve our mental well-being to ask "what-if". Every time that negative phrase creeps into your self-conscious, look at it in a different light. I accept that our path may have a few pitfalls along the way, and "what-if" one of those pitfalls places you terribly behind your personal time table of what you want to accomplish?

Instead of saying "what-if," tell yourself "so what" with

a loud and commanding tone. It's your timetable. You have the ability to adjust it, change it, or completely throw it out.

I know now that "what-if" questions are meant to be the guides along the way. It's part of our conscious awareness and natural, protective instinct. If you're trekking into the wilderness without a backpack full of necessities, you're asking for trouble.

Just take a look at this list of necessities:

- water
- food
- materials to start a fire
- emergency shelter
- flares and tools
- sunscreen
- map and compass
- first-aid supplies
- protective clothing

Without these items you might find yourself unprepared, which can result in feeling out of control. It's the same feeling that occurs when we don't get what we want. But doesn't that simple statement sound a bit childish? Let's think about it…what we want. What about turning that statement on its heel and instead realize it's not *what* we want for our lives, it's *how* we want to live our lives.

Granted, we all want better lives. But better is different to different people. One thing that we can accept and has been proven is that creativity equates to more satisfaction. **If you are not finding your creative flow, realize that like a flowing river, you can't grasp and hold onto the water. You can merely follow it and take the occasional drink.**

. . .

TO FIND YOUR CREATIVITY...

> *Banish negative thoughts and phrases such as "if-*
> *only" and "what-if".*
> *Be consciously aware that every change and new*
> *direction is an opportunity.*
> *Be prepared to grasp the creative inferences that might*
> *flit in front of us as subtlety as a firefly around*
> *the campfire.*

10

Expectations

I've talked about being a grown-up and accepting that we all have responsibilities. You are probably reading this book because you've been bit by the dream — the one where you can pursue your creative endeavor solely and live quite comfortably doing so.

You have expectations about what your life will be like if you were only a creative and not having to do your current job. Let's talk about expectations in greater detail. It's a word that comes with two sides of the coin — placing hope and responsibility on equal footing.

If you go to a fine restaurant you have certain expectations. Perhaps white tablecloths, soft lighting, better food than you get at lesser expensive restaurants and service that jumps to attention at the merest glance to the waiter.

Now let's look at the expectations of the restaurant's staff. They expect customers who are well-dressed and courteous, who pay their bill in full and display good manners.

If the food or service doesn't live up to the guests' expectations they might complain either in person or via an online review. Similarly, if the guest is rude to the staff or displays inappropriate behavior at their own table, they may be asked to leave.

You can see how expectations go both ways in this simple, everyday example. So why is it that when people pursue a creative endeavor they seem to only have expectations that their life would be so much better if only they were doing their dream job?

I had the privilege of working with a talented screenwriter named Tracey Noonan. She submitted a script to my company, which attracted my attention and I worked to get it optioned by a production company. What set Tracey apart from many screenwriters and made her such a great client was that she didn't stop pursuing her writing simply because I was working to sell her first screenplay.

She practiced the wise and I will add, the successful quality, of living without expectation. She didn't wait for the first script to sell with any expectation that she would become rich and never have to work again. The main reason was that she loved her creative craft. She didn't, nor couldn't stop being creative. And, she didn't have expectations that an acceptance from me would in turn lead to an acceptance from a production company, leading to a studio coming on board and then leading to financing and a distribution deal. She knew how many steps to the finish line there were and she decided to keep walking the walk by continuing her writing as well as other creative endeavors. In short, she acted without expectation.

Pursuing your creative endeavors in this manner isn't easy, but it's the surest way to success because you keep going like the little engine who could. The same was true for Tracey.

About two years later something remarkable occurred. Tracey and her daughter, Dani, turned a hobby into a business. They were both passionate about baking — another creative endeavor — and had dreamed up a clever idea of how to ship their homemade cupcakes and still keep them fresh and beautifully presentable. They started shipping them in mason jars and brought the idea to Shark Tank. Wicked Good Cupcakes captured the attention of Mr. Wonderful and a business was launched.

Back to expectation…now with the success of Wicked Good Cupcakes being broadcast on a network television, Tracey could have thought she was on easy street with funding coming her way. Only now, Mr. Wonderful had expectations and so did all of her new customers.

There will always be someone who holds expectations about your performance, starting with yourself. As a professional, your job is to manage your own expectations while meeting those of the people around you.

Tracey was always a hard worker, tirelessly writing until her script wasn't just good enough, but great. She showed passion and discipline, which are paramount traits needed for success. The irony is that Wicked Good Cupcakes became so successful it required all of her attention. Otherwise, I have no doubt that the world would also know Tracey as an accomplished writer because she never stopped working.

***

An Interview with Tracey Noonan

Tracey Noonan is the Founder and President of the nationally recognized Wicked Good Cupcakes.

MW: We met via the screenwriting world. How have creative pursuits shaped your life? In other words, do you feel that creativity is an integral part of your personal happiness?

TN: Absolutely. I consider myself a bit of a Fringe Dweller in that I get bored very easily and I'm constantly needing to feed my desire to "make something." A prime example of this would be last weekend while driving home from the grocery store, I had these words in my mind that were coming across as lyrics for a song.

When I got back home, I quickly penned them down and went upstairs to our music room where my husband was watching the football game. I showed him the lyrics and asked him to write a riff. When he had the chords I liked, I sent the arrangement to a friend of ours who is a guitarist and musician and he is now working on building the song from there.

Part of the danger that comes with my personality is that I'm an awesome starter, but not a great finisher. Especially if I'm depending on someone else to support whatever it is I'm working on.

MW: Do you feel that launching Wicked Good Cupcakes was somehow an offshoot of earlier creative pursuits and if so, how?

TN: Wicked Good definitely fed my need to sculpt and design. Our cupcakes (pre mason jar) had very intricate fondant decorations. My daughter, Dani, and I love art and this business was the perfect fit for us. We could be creative and sell a commodity that showcased our creative side.

MW: If there were any struggles along the way in launching Wicked Good Cupcakes what were they and how did you find the mental clarity/strength to keep pushing forward?

TN: For me, it was my pride and the feeling that failure was not an option. The money we invested to start the business wasn't a huge amount ($30,000) but it was still a lot of money for us. I knew in order to survive we would need to be "creative" with our problem solving and find ways to make things work given the financial resources we had. That's really how the idea of cupcakes in a mason jar came about. We needed to find a better way to ship our product.

MW: Do you think it's important for people who pursue a creative profession to also have business know-how? How do you personally find balance in your busy life? What balls do you need to keep in the air?

TN: Look, the bottom line is this. If you're not making

money, if no one is buying your product and if you don't have the time to dedicate to this endeavor you've got to accept the fact that this isn't the right gig for you. There's something out there for everyone. The key is being able to find what you can be the best in the world at, and make money.

My balance comes from my outside life and hobbies. I love language and I'm learning to speak Italian right now. It's a challenge which I love and hopefully will be useful to me at some point. I dream of living in a foreign country for a year (bucket list) and I dream of being totally immersed in another culture.

I also play the drums. Music is so healing and the perfect distraction for me. Then there are my three Boston terriers…Need I say more?

11

Distractions and Multitasking

I used to multi-task with a flourish, proudly boasting about how much I could do at one time. Trust me, I had mad skills that would have enthralled circus-goers or at the very least gotten a round of polite applause. I had perfected the art of feeding my dogs while making my children's lunches during which time I would make notes about my latest blog ideas and simultaneously answer emails. And yet, this is why I dumped multi-tasking.

I had reached the tipping point, that boiling over crazy zone when I forgot to do things that should never be forgotten. Shhh, don't spread this around, but one day a few years back I actually forgot to pick up my youngest from school. I was so embarrassed and ashamed that I pretended to be my twin sister when I received a disapproving stare from the school office attendant. Note: I don't have a twin sister.

So I started to wonder if I wouldn't be better off with more focus. I realized that I should put the lessons I learn in my yoga practice into daily practice with regards to the rest of my life. In short, I was going to strive to "be present." That's yoga-speak for not multi-tasking.

And guess what? I haven't found that I accomplish less

in the day. The kids' lunches still get made. The dogs get fed, although they wait until after sack lunches are set aside. My emails are answered and I have more time for reading my clients' work since I only check those emails once an hour rather than jump to them every time my computer dings.

With more focus and less multi-tasking I'm also calmer and better suited to tackle the more challenging aspects of my job. (Ever try to read a legal contract while doing squats? I wouldn't suggest it.)

If you're a multi-tasker, why not jot down your must-do jobs and then systematically tackle each one — separately. I bet you'll end your week with a clean slate and a fresh outlook. If you're a writer tackling a new project, this is imperative.

In order to get into your writing zone and turn out your creative best, you must cut yourself off from the world — at least for a short period of time. One of the biggest invasions of our time is social media. Instagram, Snapchat, Facebook, Twitter and the rest. They're addictive and fun, social and great for keeping in touch, innovative and wonderful for shoestring budget promotions, but they suck away your time and might I add, your creativity.

CUT YOURSELF OFF FROM THE WORLD...AT LEAST temporarily

AS MY CLIENT, AUTHOR LIZZY FORD, SAYS, "YOU NEED TO go into your writing cave." Lizzy is a wildly prolific author turning out four full length novels a year to a rabid audience of loyal followers who will hunt her down if she doesn't deliver. She never disappoints them.

So as Lizzy suggests, crawl into that creative cave and stay there, cut off from the world, until you feel that your creative efforts bear enough fruit that you deserve a coffee break. Notice I said "deserve." You need to put in a good effort or you won't feel good about yourself.

You are reading this book because you agree that being creative will lead to a happier you. Now, you need to jump into that zone with both feet. You've learned to overcome a fear of failure. You now understand the benefits of creativity on your mental health. It's time to adopt a habit of creative perseverance, which will reinforce your self-belief that you can do this. You are capable of creative greatness.

I know this from years of teaching adults of all backgrounds and professions. It's a matter of ripping off a band-aid. Starting a project, launching back into one after taking a break, or even figuring out the ending is not always easy, but it's necessary. When you've accomplished it, the healing begins.

Spending time on social media during your designated creative time is different from spending time reading blog posts or articles. The first is procrastination. Stay away from social media, television, your smart phone and computer while you create.

However, the second can arguably be called research. Writer's block is almost always a matter of not knowing where our story should go. Sometimes research is the key to getting "unstuck" but within a reasonable time constraint.

WHEN RESEARCH TURNS TO PROCRASTINATION

STUDYING UP ON THE TIME PERIOD OF A STORY, THE clothes that people wore, even the food and favorite pastimes, can serve to spark our imagination and get it back on track. But be warned that research can also become habitual and turn into procrastination. One should opt for balance that leans toward the writing side. Let's break it down into the most simple of processes.

Let's assume you're a busy person as most of us are, but you have found an extra hour in every day for your new project. You should spend forty-five minutes of that hour in serious creative mode, whether that is writing, painting, composing, choreography…you understand my point. The remaining fifteen minutes is your research or inspiration time. This doesn't have to be fifteen minutes straight. The more time you can spend on the serious creating, the better.

So if you are a choreographer and get stuck, perhaps you listen to music for inspiration and research. Allot yourself fifteen minutes and no more. If all goes well, you may listen to a three minute passage of music and then find the inspiration to return to your own project. That means before your hour is up, you still have another twelve minutes for further research.

But let's not get greedy and bank those inspiration hours. If you didn't use them during that hour, consider yourself ahead of the game. This isn't about keeping score. It's about setting a goal and continually moving toward that finish line while also enjoying the journey as it comes into fruition.

12

Opportunity vs Obstacles

O pportunity without hesitation. It's when a situation and a personality trait align for exceptional results. If you've ever watched a professional soccer match you'll see examples of opportunity without hesitation. It's what happens when one side loses the ball and the other team makes a run for it. The state of play changes in a matter of seconds and without having time to think or consider the what-ifs, the players react instinctively. They take the shot and a goal is scored. That's opportunity without hesitation. The same must happen in your life if you're meeting with someone who suddenly asks what you do for a living. That's your opportunity and without hesitation, you must pitch your creative endeavor.

To practice this takes discipline. That word brings up all sorts of emotions. Some imagine naughty school children standing in front of the classroom having to write sentences of remorse repeatedly. Or, if someone says they lead a disciplined life, we often think that is synonymous with "going without." No sweets, no carbs, no alcohol. It's no wonder that some people think discipline means no fun.

I don't see the term discipline in either of these lights and I don't want you to think of it like that either. To me, discipline is what will bring you ultimate happiness. It's what can lead you to good health, financial responsibility, and your creative dreams.

You can't create luck, but you can capitalize on it.

Simply writing a book will not guarantee you a publishing deal. But, you can attend writers' conferences and potentially meet an agent who compliments you on that truly amazing outfit you're wearing (that's right, being prepared is not just about having business cards, you need to look the part of a professional too) and now a conversation has been struck up.

You don't want to pitch yourself immediately. Remember your manners. Practice the rules of superior communication. Ask the agent what he is looking to find. Get him to talk about himself. Then, just maybe his needs match your genre and you can coquettishly say that his wish list sounds a great deal like your latest book. You've created an opportunity, but to do so requires discipline.

An opportunity like the one described above will not happen while watching "Bachelor" on your couch — although that's a great way to get inspired if you're creating a mean girl character. You have to be a go-getter and that means going to events, meeting people, and yes, stepping outside your comfort zone. It sounds scary, but I have a secret. It's the unknown that is scary. If you attend a networking event every month, I promise that with each passing month it becomes less scary, perhaps even natural.

When (notice I don't believe in saying 'If') the opportunity to tell someone what you are pursuing in your free time arises, you may feel silly at first, but soon, you will perfect your pitch and the nagging voice of doubt will be replaced with hope and optimism. If you are passionate about your pursuit, other people will gravitate to you and become inspired by your enthusiasm.

Discipline is also about keeping to a schedule that will allow you to meet your goals. I always lament that the one thing nobody can give me is time. This is true for everyone. Some writers/artists make the process of turning out their craft look so easy. Some books are written with simple prose that makes one think, "I could've done that." Yet, making something look easy is much harder than it seems. The true secret is to work through the writers' block that inevitably strikes.

James Herriot was such an author...

Herriot was the type of author others would aspire to be like. His stories seemed so familiar, as if he were simply re-telling his years of experience as a veterinarian. He was well known for his beloved dog stories particularly, "All Creatures Great and Small," which later became a massive television hit in Britain. These heartwarming stories, told in simple prose, described ailing animals and their owners as well as the veterinarians of North Yorkshire who would make house calls at all hours of the day or night.

One might think from reading his stories that writing about his former profession came easy to Herriot. Although he once said, "I love writing about my job because I loved it, and it was a particularly interesting one when I was a young man. It was like holidays with pay to me," he also admitted that writing the "simple prose" for how his work was described was never as simple as it appeared.

Perhaps he became so successful because he regularly transferred experiences and memories onto paper. Even in his early days working as a vet, he kept a notebook and would record the details of his treatments, not only the sicknesses of animals, but the fussiness of their owners. When he returned home after his work day, he would tell the stories to his family at dinner time and then afterwards when the kids were watching television, he would return to his notebooks.

But it wasn't until the age of 53, that he decided to formally write his experiences into stories. Working on a typewriter, he began to write. At the time of his death in 1995 at age 78, James Herriot produced dozens of best-selling books for St. Martin's Press with more than 60 million copies of his books in print.

James Herriot worked his day job and still managed to create his beloved and best-selling stories.

His life's work is a testament to both the ability to do something if you put your mind to it as well as the need to manage your time wisely.

Ideas for stories are all around us. You might overhear something amusing or maybe what you overhear makes you roll your eyes and think that's something the antagonist in your story would say. Do as the great James Herriot did and keep a notebook at the ready.

We live in a more modern world than James Herriot did. I doubt many of those reading this book would write their own stories on a typewriter. Still, there is a distinct lesson to be learned from the way James Herriot crafted his stories. Having a physical notebook or if you don't mind the small screen, the notes section of your smart phone, should be something you reach for every time you leave your computer and go out into the world. The ideas are everywhere, but they're fleeting; don't trust them to your memories.

Justin Bieber: A Lesson in Finding Opportunity
From Home Videos to Music Success

THE POPULAR STORY IS THAT CANADIAN BORN JUSTIN Bieber was discovered on YouTube and went on to release a debut album that went platinum in the United States, Canada and the United Kingdom. What about how he lived his life prior to that YouTube release?

Bieber naysayers would like to believe that luck had a hand at his discovery. However, there are plenty of people with talent who don't get discovered. Bieber was more than a singing sensation. In addition to singing, he also played drums, piano, guitar, and trumpet. That's not all. He combined showcasing his talent with unstoppable marketing and networking.

Entering a local singing competition, he took home second place honors. Afterwards, his mother uploaded the video of the competition to YouTube for friends and family to view. Uploading one video did not make the difference as far as Bieber getting discovered, but it did plant the seed in his family's mind for what was possible. His mother created a Justin Bieber channel and continued to upload his home performances. Slowly, his popularity grew and subscribers beyond their immediate circle started to follow him. Marketing executive Scooter Braun stumbled upon one of those videos and convinced Bieber's mother to visit Atlanta where Bieber would later audition for Usher and Island Def Jam Music Group, solidifying his future.

Bieber took to Twitter and connected with his new found fan base. While some celebrities turn over their social media accounts to managers, Bieber continued to take an active role in his social media coverage. Today, his account boasts over 88 million followers.

13

Create a Sense of Purpose

Tony Wagner, Innovation Education Fellow at Harvard's Technology & Entrepreneurship Center and author of "Creating Innovators: The Making of Young People Who Will Change the World," lectures regularly on the benefits of creativity.

> "Imagining and creating give us a sense of purpose, Wagner says. If you lack those things, a pervasive sense of emptiness becomes the default. The great seduction later in life is that many of us fill the vacuum with false friends, material items, and medication — both legal and otherwise."

Following your creative dreams can sometimes place you on an unconventional path and choosing to remain there may not be easy. Yet consider the truth that the things in our lives that are most worthwhile are not always the easiest to come by. Similarly, one must balance short-term with long-term goals.

In the short term, it might be easier to follow the proven

path — where you currently reside. Yet, the struggles you deal with along the way of your creative path could very well result in happier, more satisfying long-term results. Are you looking for stability today or are you seeking deeper happiness and satisfaction for tomorrow and into the future?

Achieving a Full Color Life that is creative and balanced with long-term satisfaction requires a combination of self-discipline and self-belief. While it might not be easy to cultivate these skills, once you do, they seamlessly work together.

TRY THIS EXERCISE TO NURTURE A SELF-DISCIPLINED ETHIC steeped in self-belief.

YOUR GOAL

First, write out your goal in one simple sentence. This is important. Take the time to figure out succinctly what you really want. For example, you might say, "I want to become a best-selling author."

STEPS FOR ACHIEVEMENT

Second, consider three basic steps that lead to achievement of your goal. Take the time to systematically break down the goal into the most basic of lead-in steps. You know the answer to this deep down. For instance, if we're looking at the best-selling author goal, one knows that you can't achieve this without first writing a darn good book. You'll need publicity to get the word out. You'll need positive reviews.

CREATE YOUR PERSONAL MANTRA

Third, focus on just one of the steps for achievement. Remember that self-discipline and self-belief turn creative dreams into reality. It's time to create your personal mantra using the words "discipline" and "belief".

Here is one from the example I've been describing: "I am disciplined to write every day. I believe I have a worthy story." If you are an artisan, your mantra might sound something like this: "I am disciplined to work on my craft (ie: candy, jewelry, painting, etc.) every day. I believe that I have a worthy product."

REFLECTION

Finally, using our rainbow metaphor, find a place for reflection. Whether you are in a room alone or even better, standing in front of a mirror. State your mantra aloud. Now, state it like you mean it. Be strong, be definitive and say it like you don't care who hears you. What's the worst thing that can happen if you are overheard? Remember when I discussed the children at pre-school who paint with abandon and proudly hold up their pictures? They want everyone to see it. They believe in themselves. It's time that you did the same.

WILL FERRELL: A LESSON IN PURPOSE AND PERSEVERANCE
From Morning Announcements to Acting Success

AS A STUDENT AT UNIVERSITY HIGH SCHOOL IN IRVINE, California, Will Ferrell used to make the daily morning announcements in disguised voices. This comedic habit along with occasionally doing skits over the intercom led to his interest in performing, but the road was a long one.

While at U.S.C. sometimes he would show up at friends' classes dressed as a janitor, yet a career in comedy didn't come immediately. After graduation he worked as a hotel valet and a bank teller; later he earned a job at a weekly cable show, but the love of comedy stayed with him.

He pursued comedy by giving performances at local comedy clubs and college coffee houses, and then enrolled in improvisational comedy classes held by The Groundlings, a Los Angeles theater group. Eventually, he was included in the performing troupe, which opened up other auditions including a successful one for Saturday Night Live.

Today, he is one of the highest paid actors and at the time of this writing has 98 acting credits and 53 producing credits to his name.

Part II

Refraction - Full Color Health

"To keep the body in good health is a duty...
otherwise we shall not be able to keep our mind
strong and clear." — Buddha

14

Full Color Diet

I'm not a dietician, but I've worked hard to educate myself on healthy eating habits. The suggestions I give are not meant to be looked upon as professional dietary advice, but rather, a no-nonsense, common sense approach to how healthy eating can improve your creative output.

If you consider your productive days versus your non-productive days, I'm willing to bet there's a correlation between what you eat and how you feel. We already know that our mental status contributes to our creativity. When we feel good about ourselves, maintain a sense of self-belief, allow ourselves to indulge in dreams and work to make those a reality, we tend to realize the goals we've set for ourselves. It's obvious that feeling good mentally is only part of the picture. We need to feel good physically as well, and a healthy diet is the first step.

It's impossible to concentrate when one is hungry. Feeding ourselves is such a simple solution to writer's block or any creative block, and yet, we rarely consider the importance of our diet on our productivity. Let's make it simple…

Food is fuel for our body. You wouldn't expect your car to run on empty, why should your body? The Harvard Business Review notes, "Food has a direct impact on our cognitive performance. Just about everything we eat is converted by our body into glucose, which provides the energy our brains need to stay alert. When we're running low on glucose, we have a tough time staying focused and our attention drifts."

However, just reaching for anything within grasp is not sufficient. What you eat is as important as eating in itself. Since we've just learned that most food converts to glucose in our body, it stems to reason that we don't need to consume a large amount of food that is already high in glucose. This includes carbs such as pasta, bread, cereal, and the one that so many people keep within reach…soda. If you do just one thing for your body, let it be to eliminate soda from your diet. Think of it as another four-letter word. There, I've had my rant. Let's continue.

These foods release glucose quickly, which will give you a burst of energy, but it's followed by a severe decrease in energy. Similarly, foods that are high in fat (think cheese, french fries, and pizza) may provide more sustained energy, but our digestive system must work harder to process them, which will again make us feel tired by reducing oxygen levels in the brain.

Some people try to jump on the latest bandwagon health craze, but be forewarned that some "healthy" alternatives are anything but good for you. Case in point are some of the gluten-free snacks like gluten-free muffins. Many of these contain gluten-free replacement products that are high in sugar, unhealthy oils and refined grains like corn starch or tapioca starch. Not only are these low in essential nutrients, but they lead to rapid spikes in blood sugar.

So what's the alternative? Try to create dishes that are vibrant with green, orange and purple. Even while eating, try to remember the imagery of a rainbow.

HERE ARE SOME COLORFUL FOODS THAT SHOULD FIND their way into your diet.

GREEN (BROCCOLI):

Broccoli contains the vitamins A, C and K. The health benefits are that broccoli can lower cholesterol, positively impact our body's detoxification system and due to being a rich source of kaempferol, it can also lessen the impact of allergy-related substances on our body.

ORANGE (CARROTS):

Carrots are packed with beta-carotene, which converts to vitamin A and is known to be good for our eyes. Additionally, studies have shown carrots reduce the risk of lung cancer, breast cancer, and colon cancer.

PURPLE (BEETS):

Beets are high in immune-boosting vitamin C, fiber, and important minerals like potassium, which is essential for healthy nerve and muscle function, and manganese, which is good for your bones, liver, kidneys, and pancreas. Beets also contain the B vitamin folate, which helps reduce the risk of birth defects.

BLUE (BLUEBERRIES):

Blueberries help lower our risk of heart disease by being high in fiber, potassium, folate, vitamin C, and vitamin B6.

. . .

"RAINBOW" FOODS BENEFIT THE BODY BY:
- Fighting inflammation
- Improving calcium absorption
- Lowering LDL cholesterol (the "bad" cholesterol)
- Boosting the immune system
- Improving digestion for the GI tract
- Acting as anti-carcinogens
- Reducing tumor growth
- Limiting the activity of cancer cells throughout
the body

MY HEALTHY EATING RULES

IT'S NOT OFTEN THAT A BOOK ON CREATIVITY OR WRITING
will include any mathematics, but I simply must use this
example to hammer home my point about why we must eat
healthily if we want to nurture productive creativity.

See if you remember this simple, transitive relationship:

If $a = b$ and $b = c$, then $a = c$.

Let's apply it to this chapter.

If a rainbow diet = good health and good health =
productive creativity, then a rainbow diet = productive
creativity.

So, no arguing. First and foremost, eat your veggies.
And, keep my other four healthy eating rules in the forefront
of your mind.

1. MAKE YOUR EATING DECISIONS BEFORE YOU GET
hungry.

One of the reasons that we don't make smart eating
choices is because we wait until we're super hungry to eat.

When your stomach is growling, you are at your lowest point in terms of energy and self-control. You're likely to eat the first thing you see and chances are, it won't be a good choice. Plan out your meals, particularly if you're going to a restaurant. I even look online at menus and make my decision before I arrive. More importantly, sometimes I avoid looking at the menu in the restaurant in order to stick to my guns about my earlier, healthy choice.

2. AVOID LARGE MEALS.

It's better to graze throughout the day. Spikes and drops in blood sugar are both bad for productivity and bad for the brain. Smaller, more frequent meals maintain your glucose at a more consistent level than relying on a midday feast.

3. AVOID THE INTERIOR AISLES OF THE MARKET.

Did you see the movie "Sausage Party"? Do you see what those foods get up to when we're not looking? If that's not enough reason to avoid the interior aisles, consider this fact. Foods high in fat, sugar, and salt reside in the middle. Stick with the fruits and vegetables, protein, and dairy found on the perimeter.

4. REACH FOR FRUITS AND VEGGIES THROUGHOUT the day.

Speaking of those luscious fruits…these are the snacks that you should gravitate toward. I know some modern diets tell you to avoid high fructose fruits such as apples, cherries, mangoes, watermelon and pears. But given the alternative — processed sugar — I prefer the stuff that grows on trees.

· · ·

5. NEVER EAT LATE AT NIGHT.

This practice not only puts weight on you, it interferes with your sleep pattern by making the body work hard to digest when it's supposed to be in unwind mode.

FINAL THOUGHTS ON EATING...

I DON'T BELIEVE IN DIETS. THE WORD HAS A NEGATIVE connotation and rarely do people stick with something that is limiting. Instead, I like to experiment with food. I love to cook and yes, I love to bake, but I do so in moderation. When I do bake, I try to find new ways to approach desserts that are healthier alternatives, but still delicious and satisfying. Try my quinoa brownie recipe below. You'll be surprised that it's pretty darn delicious.

TO ME, EATING SHOULD BE DONE IN THE SAME WAY WE approach books.

> *I sample different genres.*
> *I relish in the language.*
> *I return to the authors who are talented.*
> *In terms of food, this means...*
> *I eat the rainbow.*
> *I savor my food instead of grabbing and going.*
> *I return to what's good for me and avoid the junk.*

I DIDN'T ALWAYS EAT AS HEALTHILY AS I DO NOW. I USED to love carbs. One of my favorite pasta dishes was fettuccine

alfredo, loaded in butter and cream. My coffee was a deca-
dent treat with a spoonful of brown sugar and half & half.
But, I can honestly say that the conscious change I made to
improve my diet has done so much more than simply to
improve my appearance.

I sleep better at night. I have more energy in the day. I
feel happier.

I still love my morning coffee, but I've learned to love it
without brown sugar and I now substitute coconut creamer
for my old half and half habit.

I'm by no stretch perfect, and I do take indul-
gences. But, I reserve those for special occasions and if
I attend a party, I ensure that I eat very carefully in
the days prior. Just as we must be disciplined with our
creative pursuits, so must we be in our personal
practices.

QUINOA BROWNIES, ADAPTED FROM A RECIPE BY GIADA De Laurentiis

(makes 12 muffin sized desserts or 24 mini ones)
1 stick unsalted butter
1 1/4 cups mini chocolate chips
1/2 cup sugar
2 eggs
1 1/2 teaspoons vanilla
1/4 teaspoon almond extract
1/2 cup flour
1/2 cup quinoa flour
mini marshmallows
muffin tin liners

Pre-heat oven to 350 degrees. Line your muffin tin with
liners.

Melt the butter in a saucepan. Remove from heat and

add half the mini chocolate chips (3/4 cup). Stir until melted.

Combine the sugar and eggs. Add the melted chocolate to the egg mixture and whisk until fully combined. Add vanilla and almond extracts. Then add the flours. Finally, add the remaining chocolate chips.

Spoon mixture into muffin liners and top with about five mini marshmallows.

Bake for 10-12 minutes. These delicious bites will be gooey in the center while they're warm, like a molten chocolate cake, but healthier!

An Interview with Lisa Douthit

Lisa Douthit is the author of the Amazon #1 bestselling book "Wellness Warrior: Fighting for Life in Fabulous Shoes". Her creative journey has given her the stamina and strength to fight four battles with cancer. She has extensively researched how diet, exercise, and alternative therapies benefit the immune system and one's spiritual health.

MW: How do you view creativity in your own life and what are its benefits for others?

LD: I believe that we are put on this planet as creative beings. Think about it. Have you ever watched a young child at play? Their eyes are filled with wonder as they sit on the floor for hours banging on pots and pans listening to the symphony they've created in their minds.

To me, creativity breeds freedom and empowerment. It allows me to breathe in all that life has to offer because I know I am in charge, not a victim to others' agendas. I can take ownership of my life and come up with new ways to shift something I don't like.

When I am in my creative zone, I'm open and at peace with myself and my surroundings. I look at life without judgment. All things are possible because I'm free to imagine how I want the outcome to be. Then I can create the outline for which to meet my goals.

We are all given creativity as a gift and the limitless freedom to use it however we choose. We are our only limitation. I think the biggest murderer of creativity is fear. Moving past the fear allows you to open yourself up to the infinite possibilities of life.

Without my creative mind, I would be lost and my spirit would die. Life would be bleak and depressing in its mundane drone.

Creativity doesn't just fuel my profession, it fuels my reason to get up in the morning. I get to create who I want to be each day in all facets of my life. Without creativity, I would have no tools to design my path to my future.

Without creativity, it would be impossible to fully maximize our potential because we would not be able to visualize and create our destiny.

Full Color Fitness

Have you ever noticed that you aren't as hungry for bad stuff after you exercise? This is because exercise controls your weight by increasing the number of calories your body uses for energy.

But there are so many other reasons to get moving. Consider the following findings from the Mayo Clinic:

- *Exercise improves mood*
- *Exercise combats disease and health problems*
- *Exercise boosts energy*
- *Exercise promotes sleep*
- *Exercise improves sex drive*

Yet, there's one more benefit to exercise…you guessed it. Exercise improves creativity.

A study conducted by Lorenza Colzato at Leiden University in The Netherlands found that people were able to think much more creatively if they engaged in exercise four times a week compared to those who led a sedentary lifestyle.

Many authors and other creatives find that the release of

83

endorphins that occurs during and after exercise helps to boost their creativity and unlock the brain.

Researchers have found a relationship between exercise and cognitive functioning, specifically creativity. In fact, this finding can be taken to the next level where we can use the old adage, "Is the tail wagging the dog or the dog wagging the tail?" What this means is that not only does exercise result in a creative burst of energy, but some authors and artists purposefully engage in exercise in order *to become* more creative and help overcome mental blocks and lack of inspiration.

Philosopher Henry David Thoreau stated, "The moment my legs begin to move my thoughts begin to flow…"

FINDING EXERCISE THAT SUITS YOU

WE ALL KNOW THAT EXERCISE IS GOOD FOR OUR BODIES, but to learn that it can boost your creativity is just another reason to find a fitness program that works for you. However, doing so can sometimes be as difficult as finding the right eating plan for your body and lifestyle.

Fortunately, the days of just going to a gym to jump on a treadmill are long behind us. There are a myriad of options available to us from different fitness classes to private training and even apps. The key is to find a program that you enjoy doing.

In addition to our stated reason of wanting to boost creativity and feel the rush of endorphins, there is the more obvious benefit to exercise — looking and feeling good. To start, you might want to assess your personal fitness goals.

- Do you want to build muscle?
- Do you want to increase flexibility?
- Do you want to improve endurance?

In my mind, all of the above are appropriate reasons to exercise, but I'll add one more reason that may be surprising to some...escape.

My exercise of choice is yoga in a heated room (105 degrees F). During my routine, it's the one moment of the day when I don't think of anything else. It's the perfect escape and relaxation for my mind, which is why I believe I'm more productive afterwards. I start every weekday at the studio bright and early at 7 a.m. I've been actively practicing for ten years. Prior to that, I spent my time in a dance studio, although the years of ballet were hard on my ankles, knees and hips, which is why I transferred to yoga. I find that it still provides the discipline of ballet, but with the added benefit of connecting the mind to the body.

How to Choose an Exercise Program

Larry Sarokin, fitness teacher and author of "Mudwalking: Unleash the Power of Walking for Vitality+Rejuvenation+Longevity," says, "Exercise is very personal. Choosing the best workout to achieve vitality, rejuvenation and longevity, is more about understanding yourself, your lifestyle and your life responsibilities than about mastering downward dogs, spinning cycles, or completing hundreds of crunches. You don't need to prove anything to anyone else — you want something that works for you."

To find this perfect fit, I suggest asking yourself the following questions:

1. Do you want a gym/studio based program or do you prefer being outdoors?
2. Do you want to exercise at your own pace or through an instructor led class?
3. Do you prefer a dance based program or a cross-training approach?

Tired of the same old exercise class, take a look at the sheer variety of new programs available:

- Soul Cycle
- Yoga
- Pilates
- Zumba
- Hip Hop/Funk
- Boot Camp
- Cross-Fit
- Barre
- Metabolic Conditioning (MetCon)
- SurfSet Classic
- PoundFit

How to Stick with an Exercise Program

MARK TWAIN ONCE SAID, "THE SECRET TO GETTING ahead is getting started." The same applies to exercise. Get started and feel proud in your efforts for they will benefit you — mind, body, and spirit.

One of the keys to sticking with an exercise program is to enjoy it. You might say, "I don't like to exercise." Okay, fair enough. We don't all like the same thing. But, I bet you can agree to like some form of physical activity, set to your preferred music, in a pleasing environment. Take stock of your personal likes and dislikes and then, find the program that suits you. Trust me, it's out there.

THEN, USE THESE TIPS TO STICK WITH THE PROGRAM.

1. Make a commitment to yourself.

SET A GOAL OF TRYING TO WORK OUT AT LEAST THREE times a week — Monday, Wednesday, and Friday. See how it goes and then work up to four or five days a week. Many people find that exercise can be addictive…at least it's a good addiction. The more you do it, the more you'll feel the release of endorphins and you'll want to go back.

2. SET AN APPOINTMENT AND REMINDER.

By scheduling exercise in the same manner you would a doctor's appointment, you are more likely to show up. My yoga studio has an app that allows us to check in online. I often check in the night before simply because making that commitment ensures that I won't make any excuses in the morning. It's easy to get caught up in emails and ignore the time, but if I've already logged in and said I will be there, then I'm going to be there.

3. EXERCISE WITH A FRIEND.

Similar to the point above, if you make a commitment with a friend to show up to a class, you're not likely to bail on that person. Besides, working out with a friend is fun.

JULIANNE HOUGH: A LESSON IN DISCIPLINE
  A Lifelong Pursuit of Dancing Success

MOST PEOPLE ARE FAMILIAR WITH JULIANNE HOUGH FOR her role on ABC television's "Dancing with the Stars." On the show, she became the youngest of the cast's professional dancers to take an amateur contestant to first place. In spite of what appeared to be beginner's luck as such a young face on the show, Hough actually devoted years to her dancing craft, beginning competitive dancing at just age nine.

Hough trained in many disciplines of dance including jazz, ballet, and tap as well as studied song, theatre, and gymnastics. At 12 years, she was entering dance competitions not only in the U.S., but also in the UK. She became the youngest dancer, and only American, to win both Junior World Latin Champion and International Latin Youth Champion at the Blackpool Dance Festival when she was just 15 years of age.

Her early singing training was put to good use when Hough decided to release a country single called "Will You Dance with Me." The song placed at No. 100 on the Billboard Pop 100 chart and she later signed with Universal Music Group Nashville's Mercury Nashville division. Hough won the Top New Artist award at the 44th Annual Academy of Country Music Awards in 2009.

Acting stints followed with roles in "Harry Potter and the Philosopher's Stone," "Burlesque," and "Footloose" leading to her own starring role opposite Josh Duhamel in the 2012 film "Safe Haven," based on the Nicholas Sparks' novel.

Like many artistic people, one creative endeavor led to others as Julianne continued to push herself toward excellence.

Full Color Life

16

Full Color Schedule

With the case made that happiness inspires creativity and certain activities are more likely to lead to happiness, one must also address how to fit these activities into your daily life. But perhaps you lament that there's too much on your plate?

The people highlighted in this book were busy, too. So busy in fact, that I worried about asking them to answer my questions. Yet, every person I asked, agreed to provide insight into their creative process and what led them to personal success. They were happy to offer advice that could be shared. Why? Because busy people tend to be the most successful. They know how to find balance and more importantly, they know how to prioritize. This chapter focuses on that important skill along with some insight into how busy people seem to live in a 25-hour day.

First, let's agree that we're all busy. It's easy to compete with one another about who is the busiest. Let's agree that we all have multiple work responsibilities along with commitments to relationships and then we try to carve out some 'me' time. Oh, and there's sleep. Let's not forget that one. In fact, I think it's so important, we're going to start with it.

THE IMPORTANCE OF SLEEP

BY STIMULATING YOUR IMAGINATION, YOU CULTIVATE creativity. But like your body, your imagination can't run on overdrive all of the time. It needs down time to rejuvenate itself. This is why sleep is so important. Such an easy fix and yet so many people ignore its importance.

A study conducted at the University of Lübeck in Germany found that students who faced a problem were much more likely to find a solution if they got a good night's rest. A Harvard Medical School study resulted in similar findings although the technique was different. Rather than have the students solve problems after a night's rest, they asked students to visualize their problem prior to going to sleep. Many reported answers came to them in dreams.

I see the latter study as being potentially problematic because in my book, fretting over a problem prior to bed could interfere in one's sleep. I know it may sound a bit presumptuous to suggest an alternate method to one hypothesized by Harvard, but I'm going to be that bold.

Here's my method of sleep-problem-solving. You'll recall that I've asked you to keep an idea notebook at the ready. If you're struggling with a passage in your writing or a bar of music in a composition, the choreography of a dance, or any number of creative set backs that might strike, write it down. Very simply, state the problem in your notebook prior to going to bed.

The act of writing it down ensures that you won't risk

forgetting, which I believe is what keeps many of us up at night. It's not that we can't solve a problem, it's that we fear we'll ignore the problem. Writing it down prevents this and also serves to transmit the concept via another method to our brain, thus giving us more freedom to subconsciously imagine the solution while we sleep. It's similar to the Harvard study, but without the risk of keeping you awake with worry.

Whether you are attempting to cultivate creativity by writing regularly, finding time for play, or getting a good night's rest, each of these components requires that daily time is set aside for the activity. It might sound silly to plan time for sleep, but too many of us don't get enough sleep and therefore, one must consciously make the decision of when "bedtime" should occur in order to get enough of it. This brings us to the importance of keeping a schedule, which may sound rigid and counterproductive to creativity, but I promise that you'll discover why schedules are so important to achieving your creative goals.

SETTING PRIORITIES

I'VE JUST MADE THE POINT THAT SLEEP NEEDS TO BE A priority. Without adequate sleep you can't sustain a high level of creativity because quite simply, your brain will not work at optimum capacity. Let's examine your other daily priorities as well.

Using myself as an example, I'll divide my responsibilities into three main **Priority Categories** (Family, Work, and Personal) and list the tasks that have to be completed within each one, followed by more specific **Action Items**.

. . .

FAMILY
Action Item: shopping, meal preparation, driving, homework help, time with my spouse and children

WORK
Action Item: publishing, editing, social media, correspondence, consulting, teaching, accounting

PERSONAL
Action Item: exercise, personal writing, time with friends

SETTING YOUR PRIORITY CATEGORIES AND ACTION
Items:

THE ABOVE IS MEANT TO BE MY MOST GENERAL LIST OF
responsibilities. Now it's your turn. Write a similar list for
yourself. If it works for you, feel free to copy mine (Family /
Work / Personal).

Next, write your own "action items" but don't get into
specifics just yet. By initially listing just the minimum
requirements of each responsibility, one can approach each
day more systematically without feeling overwhelmed.

I know that the most general items occur every day, but
specific action items and sub-action items, which I breakdown into individual to-do lists, might only need to be
tackled once a week.

KEEP THESE SCHEDULING TIPS IN MIND:

- Not every task has to be completed every day.
- You don't have to respond to every email as soon as it arrives.
- You can turn off social media while you're in work mode. (What a concept!)
- Avoid distractions if you are in a creative mode (note the above tip).

Your Calendar of Action Items:

IT'S IRONIC THAT CREATING A TO-DO LIST IS MEANT TO make us feel in control, but too often it results in our feeling overwhelmed. Sometimes, I even think my to-do list needs a to-do list, which is why I started to break down each item systematically into sub-action items.

I suggest you do the same for the simple reason that we all wear many hats. We take on multiple roles so it stands to reason that we benefit by "categorizing" our life. Otherwise, the responsibilities become just too great to tackle, our stress levels increase, and the resulting emotion we feel is certainly counter-intuitive to being creative.

The first step is to list each Sub-Action Item and determine whether it must be done on a daily, weekly, or (if you're so lucky) monthly basis.

LET ME ILLUSTRATE BY OUTLINING MY WORK CATEGORY and its corresponding Action Items and Sub-Action Items below.

WORK (PRIORITY CATEGORY)

Action Items = publishing, editing, social media, correspondence, consulting, teaching, accounting

SUB-ACTION ITEMS:
Publishing

- conceive and contract cover art for books
- oversee formatting for books
- editing and/or proofreading

Social Media

- conceive tweets
- conceive Facebook posts
- manage Pinterest boards

Office

- correspondance (emails)
- accounting

Consulting / Teaching

- consulting for clients
- weekly preparation and leading of classes

THERE ARE DIFFERENT METHODS FOR NOW TAKING EACH Sub-Action Item and categorizing it as a daily, weekly or monthly task. I'm a visual person so I like to print out a calendar and color code the items based on whether they are performed each day or perhaps, each week.

For instance, daily responsibilities within each Priority

Category would include those sub-action items in the Social Media and Office list. Under the Action Item of Consulting/Teaching, my weekly classes are obviously weekly Sub-Action responsibilities. Whereas, the other Work responsibilities such as those listed under Publishing are performed when a client contracts me, which may be on a weekly basis, or perhaps, monthly.

When I add my other main Category responsibilities such as Family, the daily requirements obviously change. What's important to remember when you put together your own list is to take note of what must be done *now*. Chances are not every Family or Personal responsibility needs to be completed daily, but I encourage you to move your creative endeavor if only for half and hour to one hour a day, to the daily responsibility section.

ASK A BUSY PERSON

LET'S FACE IT, THERE'S A LOT WE WANT TO DO IN THIS life. Isn't it a wonder that kids sometimes lament that they're bored? That's one thing I never experience because I'm just too busy to be bored. There are so many things I want to accomplish, but rather than get overwhelmed, I allow that energy to push me forward and achieve those dreams. You can too.

Developing a schedule will not sabotage your creativity. On the contrary, you'll create balance in your life that allows you to be an optimum partner, parent, worker, and still have time for your dreams.

Schedules can start off with broad brush strokes such as what you want to accomplish in a given month. Then, you can break those goals down into weekly to-do lists. If you're managing parenting duties with a job and then wanting to pursue your creative dreams on the side, that list then needs to be broken down by the hour.

Here's a sample of my weekly to-do list along with my daily responsibilities. Sometimes I joke that I wish I had an extra day in the week or maybe just one extra hour each day, but since I haven't yet figured out how to create the 25-hour day, I manage by being disciplined and sticking to my list.

Some people might think: schedule = boring. Repeat after me…Busy does not equate to boring. It's an impossibility. You'll see this from my schedule. By the way, I never claimed to lead a glamorous life, what I'm sharing is the truth about my life…washing dogs and tidying up included. Wearing many hats isn't necessarily the ideal way to skyrocket to the top of your field. I'm sure if I had just one responsibility — focusing only on my writings — I would certainly be more prolific. But what is certain to me is that I would not be living a Full Color Life.

Doing one thing and only one thing is not fulfilling to me. I want it all. I know that I can't have everything at once. I know that doing everything might make each one of those individual things less successful, but that's where the balance comes in.

Not every task is weighted equally. For instance, my children will always take priority over work. I have another phrase I use about my little ducklings and that is, "They aren't fully hatched." What I mean is that until they are successfully admitted to a university and living the lives that they have dreamed, I feel that my responsibilities to them are not complete. That's not to say that I turn my back on them once they hit 18 and are at university. But, at that point, the balance of duties and responsibilities in my life will once again shift and I'll be able to then give other areas of my life more time.

My Daily Schedule:

6 a.m. Wake up and do half an hour of writing

6:30 a.m. Wake up everyone else in the house, say my goodbyes and head to the yoga studio

7 - 8 a.m. Daily yoga practice

8:30 a.m. I'm home, showered, and at my desk with coffee

8:30-9 a.m. Review emails from the night before / pitch client projects to production companies

9 - 10 a.m. Social media replies and posts

10 a.m. Grab breakfast

10:15-11 a.m. Create blog posts for clients

11 a.m. to 1 p.m. Edit client books or scripts

1 p.m. Lunch

1:30- 2 Back at my desk, depending on if lunch was alone or with colleagues

2 - 3:30 p.m. More editing/writing

3:30-4 p.m. This is when I pick up my daughter from school and get her settled in with snack and homework.

4 - 5 p.m. Research — I could be researching new social media trends, production companies, or even marketing avenues for clients.

5 - 6 p.m. Editing / Publishing Duties

6 - 6:30 p.m. Homework help for my children. This can sometimes extend to 7 p.m.

7 - 8:30 Final emails and writing of the day

8:30 p.m. Bedtime for my daughter which always includes a story

8:30 - 9:30 p.m. Time with my husband catching up on one of our favorite series

9:30 - 10 p.m. Bedtime for me. I usually read for pleasure for half an hour before lights out

AN INTERVIEW WITH BRYAN COHEN

Bryan Cohen is a living walking example of if you want something done ask a busy person. He is the author of "Ted Saves the World," a YA sci-fi/fantasy series, and a collection of creative writing prompts books. His books have been downloaded over 400,000 times. He also provides education to authors on marketing strategies via his widely acclaimed site, www.sellingforauthors.com and via his podcast on self-publishing news at www.sellmorebooksshow.com.

MW: Everyone has moments of doubt or an experience with stumbling blocks. Could you describe a time when being creative pulled you out of the doldrums?

BC: When I'm working on a creative project, it's best for me to have a set time to "be creative" every single day. If I'm in a slump during that time, it's so helpful to know that I'm going to have a set hour or two where I'm going to be creating something. Whether it's good or bad, I know I'll be doing something that will eventually provide entertainment or education to someone somewhere.

While I can't think of a specific moment where creativity grabbed me by the bootstraps and pulled me up, I can vouch for the power of creativity cutting short many of those negative feelings before they become doldrum-worthy. Everyday creativity is one heck of a mood enhancer.

MW: You write fiction and non-fiction as well as teach authors marketing strategies. How do you balance the creative and business aspects of your life?

BC: Taking on multiple projects is very challenging, but when you can keep "church and state" on separate sides of the day, you can get a whole lot of work done. I try to keep my fiction and nonfiction writing in the morning when I'm feeling the most creative. Business and teaching goes in the afternoon, since I can buckle down and do the same sort of task (emailing, coaching, calls) for a few hours at a time.

Planning and batching have also been incredibly helpful. By planning ahead, things don't catch me off guard, pulling me out of something important for an urgent, but less important task. Batching a series of emails I need to write or any other kind of repetitive project helps me to stay in the same "mode" without having to switch back and forth. When I do my copywriting, I try to write three or four book descriptions in a single sitting, as opposed to editing each description individually and sending it out. I write them in a row, edit them in a row, collate them in a row, and send them in a row. I batch as many of these tasks together as possible to help me to be as efficient with my time as I can be.

MW: How is it personally beneficial (ie: mentally/spiritually) to wear both of these hats (being a creative/being a businessman)?

BC: Creativity is awesome, but it's not always good at selling itself. By wearing my business hat, I get to make sure my creative work gets out into the world. If I was just business-focused, I might not have anything good to put out there. By wearing both, I get the best of both worlds. I wouldn't recommend trying to wear them at the same time though. Wear your creative hat part of the day, and your business hat the other part.

MW: I hear that you've even worked as an actor. Explain why creative people seem to be able to juggle multiple balls/interests? What drives you to pursue different creative endeavors and how is your life better as a result of it?

BC: I think part of it has to do with training your brain to be versatile. Actors and improvisers have to keep several things going at once. Actors need to remember their lines, internalize how they're personalizing the scene (making it fit somehow with something in their own lives or experience), and connect with the other actors all at the same time. I think doing work like that almost makes you crave that multifaceted project that another person would turn down. I'm sure that many other creative endeavors inspire the same sort of drive.

I don't always love creating. It's hard work and there are many valleys between the hills. But, I love having created. I love sharing my work with the world and seeing the looks on peoples' faces. Everything from improv to novels to training courses have given me this sensation in different ways. When you get beyond the "what if I did this" stage and actually create something, it's one hell of a feeling. I strive to feel that feeling now and in the future. That's one of the things that drives me to create.

It's also a very consumer focused world. We're encouraged from all angles to consume, and in many ways, discouraged from creating. Fighting the haters and making something you're proud of is an impressive feat. I love being able to contribute to the creator-side and I hope to be able to do it for the rest of my life.

17

Full Color Relationships

W e've just discussed how to balance our vast responsibilities. Note that I don't like using the term 'juggle' that has become so popular in recent years. To me, the connotation is off. Inevitably, when you juggle, the ball will eventually drop. That's different from balance, which if handled with mindfulness, will continue.

To find balance in our lives, our relationships are an integral force. As such, our relationships are something to be nurtured with careful attention paid to them each day. Our relationships are made up of various groups to include:

- Immediate family
- Extended family
- Friends
- Social Groups (ie: sports teams, places of worship)
- Business

Perhaps, not every relationship will need attention on a daily basis, but certainly for the benefit of our physical and mental health, I would assume that at least two of these would become a daily priority in your life, alternating between the list.

The fact that we wear many hats in terms of responsibilities is never more evident than in the various facades we wear in front of our circle of relationships. During holidays when we inevitably spend more time around extended family, many people speak of stress. The same applies to our business relationships during times when deadlines must be met. This is a book that focuses on creativity. It's not meant to be a life guide for mending a family relationship that was sullied because of an incident that occurred over a decade ago. Yet, I'm a firm believer that stress not only interrupts our ability to be creative, but can even prevent it.

Experts say there's a strong connection between creative expression and overall well-being. Key components of the creative personality, like novelty-seeking and perseverance, are also good predictors of life satisfaction. Therefore, for the sake of your creative well-being, it's important to acknowledge that your relationships will affect it. It is therefore important for your overall health to work on your relationships, address problems from the past, and go forward with the intention of being a positive component within each relationship group. One way to achieve this is through play.

PLAY...AN ESSENTIAL LIFE SKILL

PLAYING WITH YOUR ROMANTIC PARTNER, FRIENDS, CO-workers, pets, and children can fuel your imagination, spark creativity, assist with problem-solving, and ensure your emotional well-being.

Being an adult and playing are not in opposition to each

other. In fact, it's important to develop a method of play with all of your relationships. Granted, the method and degree of play is different. For instance, you wouldn't suggest going outdoors to throw a frisbee with a co-worker, but you might with your child. However, if you're unsure of what constitutes play in the business world, it's as simple as connecting to someone with a joke or sharing a funny (albeit appropriate) story.

Regardless of which relationship you are with, focus your play on the goal of simply having fun and enjoying yourself. The goal does not have to be anything beyond those two simple characteristics.

With friends, play could be going out for lunch. With children, it could be dressing up or going to the park. With your spouse, it could be going for a walk. Play is not a pointless activity that takes time from your varied responsibilities. It's necessary and by making time for play, you give yourself permission to jumpstart creativity. It also boosts brain functioning if your form of play is puzzles or a game of chess. It relieves stress by giving us a burst of endorphins.

Yet too often, adults don't know how to play, even if they wanted to try it. Sadly, from the time we are teens, we're told to "grow up" if we act silly. We learn that taking responsibility is an admirable quality, and certainly it is. However, being responsible is a necessary commitment we owe ourselves as well as others. Learning to play as an adult is necessary for your creative well-being. Let's look at two examples of how to easily incorporate play time into your adult life.

PLAY OUTDOORS

· · ·

PEOPLE OFTEN FIND THAT A SURPLUS OF CREATIVE IDEAS come to them when they're on vacation. It's no wonder. You're outside your normal work grind. You're relaxed. Perhaps you're even taking time to play. This is the perfect time for the creative spark to be ignited. So why not recreate this when you need it?

Take the time for play and relaxation. One simple way is via my earlier discussion on exercise. Not a fan of structured classes or the gym atmosphere? Take time to get back to nature. Go out and walk. You just need a pair of tennis shoes and a day without rain. (Can you tell I'm a native Californian? I'm sure those who live in the mid-west are calling me a softie by now.)

Still not feeling a spark of inspiration? Let nature guide you. Research suggests that time spent outdoors boosts creativity. Take photographs, sketch, or spend time outdoors listening to music. The simple act of removing yourself from the confines of your desk is often all you need to get inspired. Just don't make the mistake of going on a nature hike without a way to write down your amazing ideas.

Getting back to nature is a phrase adults have coined when they want to get away from it all, specifically their day job. Yet its roots come from when we were children and spent more time playing outdoors. The creative advantages that come from cultivating childlike wonder are as numerous as getting back to our young roots and playing outdoors.

PLAY WITH CHILDLIKE WONDER

TO PLAY IS TO BE CHILDLIKE, WHICH IS NOT SOMETHING that comes naturally to most adults. After all, even when we're children we're told to "grow up" and "act maturely." So now that you're an adult, I'm going to lament that you need to act like a child once in awhile for the sake of your creative endeavors.

The easiest way to do this is a similar tactic I use when I'm stuck with a plot point in a novel. I ask myself questions. If my character is on a journey, but as a writer I've lost the point, I ask myself aloud, "What does my character want? What is their purpose?" Somehow, by verbalizing the question, an assortment of potential answers becomes more clear.

A similar method can be conducted to find your inner child. Ask yourself what I call "a wonder question." For instance:

- "I wonder what my dog thinks when I..."
- "I wonder what the neighbors do when nobody is watching..."
- "I wonder where I would go when I learn to fly..."

Play Your Way to Improved Relationships

As a method for keeping relationships fresh, play is your go-to tool. Play brings happiness and resilience to relationships. Through play, we can develop a closeness and trust in one another.

As a result, play can also be that necessary tool to heal past disagreements. The trust that is developed through play improves business relationships by letting us work more effectively together. Spouses who approach their relationships with play see improved intimacy.

Make a conscious effort to bring play into your relationships and all of your connections will benefit — not just with family and friends, but also those you share with co-workers.

18

Exercise the Creative Muscle

Write regularly and it becomes easier
each time.

I teach a course in novel writing and screenwriting and without fail, every semester a student will admit to me about how they often struggle to write even a sentence that they deem to be good enough. I could probably write an entire book just on that subject, but for the sake of brevity, let me assure you that writing or any creative endeavor, for that matter, becomes easier the more you do it.

If you're a runner, the first time you attempt a half marathon might feel like climbing Mount Everest. I tip my hat to people who have the stamina to keep going mile after mile. Yet those dedicated runners have told me that each one started by first tackling only one mile. After that, they added one more, and another, and another.

I reminded myself of these runners' stories when I first started traveling overseas to England. The first time I made that nine hour journey felt like a lifetime. I remember looking at the flight map and feeling like I just wanted to skydive out of that plane. I couldn't bear to sit there another minute. The next trip I surprised myself by not looking at the map until I was over New York and half way there.

Granted, sitting in one place doesn't even compare to running a marathon, but please remember that I'm not a runner and never will be. What I'm trying to explain is that it's the unknown that is most difficult for us. Once we become accustomed to what is needed to accomplish something, we are more likely to complete the task. When I finally got used to sitting in one place for nine hours, I found I was better equipped to do so without complaint.

The same applies to sitting down and writing. If you only attempt this once in a blue moon it's going to feel like a transatlantic flight. You're going to be bouncing in and out of your seat, running to the kitchen for a drink or snack, deciding that now is absolutely the time when you need to get a jump on preparing your taxes. In short, if you never write, you'll probably do anything other than sit and write.

Conversely, if you make writing a daily habit, even if you're writing time period is just fifteen minutes, you'll quickly get used to sitting and being productive for that amount of time. Soon, you'll be able to stretch your writing time and with more time put in, your productivity will go up not just in the output of material, but in its quality as well.

WRITING PROMPTS

ONE WAY TO GET YOUR CREATIVE MIND ACTIVE IS VIA writing prompts. These are scenarios that will spark your imagination. Sometimes, you can even be so lucky as to write one and have it later find its way into one of your own writing projects.

Often, all that's needed to get you unstuck is the knowledge that you are still a viable writer with ideas. Try one of these prompts developed by *Writers Digest* magazine the next time you have writer's block.

Breaking up with Writer's Block

It's time for you and Writer's Block to part ways. Write a letter breaking up with Writer's Block, starting out with, "Dear Writer's Block, it's not you, it's me …"

The One That Got Away

You bump into an ex-lover on Valentine's Day—the one whom you often call "The One That Got Away." What happens?

Mystery Cookie

You come into work and find a cookie mysteriously placed on your desk. Grateful to whoever left this anonymous cookie, you eat it. The next morning you come in and find another cookie. This continues for months until one day a different object is left—and this time there's a note.

Sent to the Wrong Printer

You're at work and you print something personal and sensitive. Unfortunately, you've sent it to the wrong printer and, by the time you realize it, someone else already scooped it up.

AFFIRMATIONS FOR THE CREATIVE

TALENT IS A TRICKY CONCEPT. SOME SAY YOU'RE BORN with it. Others say it can be developed and nurtured. I think it's a matter of both -- you must have an innate talent for your creative endeavor, but even a "natural" athlete must listen to a coach and practice regularly.

For a writer, this means reading as well as writing. The writer with a gift for words must study their craft by reading literary greats as well as current best sellers. If you're a writer who is not also a reader, you are cheating yourself from potential inspiration from new genres that you may want to take a stab at trying.

Singers must perfect their voices through lessons. Even working actors often attend workshops led by other professionals they admire. Dancers do the same. Regardless of your field, there's always someone who has earned a level of achievement that you can observe and study.

And then you put in the time working on your own craft…and heed this part…you do so every work day. At least five days a week you will go "to your office." That office might be a dancer's studio, an artist's loft, a writer's retreat, an actor's stage. No matter what your creative expression, you must work on it and work regularly so as not to allow that creative muscle to atrophy. The more regular you keep your endeavors, the easier it will be to find your flow and avoid the writer's block, dancer's rut, an artist's lapse and any other sign that creativity is taking a sick day.

Before I was a writer and book packager, I grew up in a dancer's studio. From the time I was five I was taken to ballet and by the time I was sixteen I could drive myself. I always loved the way the music inspired movement and the way dancers could tell a story and express emotion through that movement. My imagination would take flight and my own stories would percolate and brew in my mind.

Dance remained a big part of my life from childhood through my 20s. While at the ballet barre doing my daily warm-ups, my mind would start to imagine my own stories. An injury and subsequent knee surgery ended any ideas of pursuing dance full time and when I got to USC I studied communications and journalism, but my love of dance and more importantly, the desire and training to practice daily had long been instilled within me and I continued to use dance as an outlet for my physical well-being as well as a mode to send my imagination on its flight. I don't think it's coincidence that so many creative people also are very disci-

plined people who enjoy exercising their body as well as
their mind. Getting your body moving and keeping it
healthy directly impacts your mental strength and vitality.

After graduation, I accepted a full time job at an entertainment PR firm, but I still carved out time in my day (even
if that meant working at night) for work outs -- both mental
and physical. Early morning when I was fresh was for my
own personal writing. Then my day job responsibilities
would kick in. On my way home from work regardless of
the time, I'd stop at the gym or a dance studio. I knew if I
went home first, I'd get caught in the trap of feeling too
tired to go out again let alone to go out and work out. So,
gym clothes, leotard and ballet flats had a permanent resi-
dence in my car. I would eliminate any excuse for going to a
class.

Exercising the creative muscle isn't just a euphemism.
Creativity loves physical activity. Creativity loves regularity.
And, if all else fails, sometimes, you just need to remind
yourself to…

- Ponder your world.
- Dare to express your thoughts.
- Work hard but love your work.
- Find joy in the everyday.
- Live with kindness in your heart and share it
  freely.
- Be playful, but live responsibly.
- Believe in your talents and have faith in your
  future.

19

Creating Time

O ur previous discussion of writing daily will naturally lead into the conversation about maintaining a schedule. Some writers hate the idea of keeping a schedule, believing that creativity strikes when the muses are inspired, but I disagree...strongly! Being accountable is what's going to set your creativity in motion.

Even if the first attempt is less than stellar, leave it on the page and keep going. Don't stop and 'fix' something, just get the thoughts on paper. (Gosh, you should see some of my ramblings before I go back and edit, but I embrace them all the same.) The plot is the hardest part. The details of characterization and dialogue are like the icing and decorations on the cake. But you need the cake before you can add the candles and inscription.

The wise and witty Anne LaMott talked about "Shitty First Drafts," which I embrace and encourage every writer to do as well. This means you acknowledge the imperfections of your work as they occur. The goal is not to create a masterpiece straight out of the gate. It's to get your ideas down and then massage them into place later.

This is also a matter of trust and belief. Trust that your

ideas have merit. Trust in your abilities to edit and fix any problems. Believe in yourself as a creative and inspired being. When you tap into your creativity, those ideas will flow fast and freely. Don't stop that flow by fixating on the perfect adjective, the name of a character, their hair or eye color. Those are details that can be added once the story has experienced its first draft. More importantly, **work honestly**. This means you put in the time and you don't stop when it gets tough. That's when breakthroughs occur. Your details are akin to dessert and you can't have the chocolate cake if you don't eat your veggies. Excuse the dose of mom-ism; I couldn't help myself.

The point: **create fearlessly**. Don't worry if it's not good enough or even plain old, downright not good. This isn't the final draft of your novel, the final choreographed dance, or the final anything. This is the beginning. Your only goal is to brain dump every idea.

Chuck Wendig, an American author, comic book writer, screenwriter, and blogger, best known for his popular online blog, "Terribleminds," says: "There's no wrong way to do it, as long as you're doing it. There's no timetable, as long as you're taking the time."

What a great sentiment. Sometimes I wish the day was longer so I could fit everything in, but when life gets in the way of your creative endeavors, that's when you remind yourself that as long as you are devoting some time…any time…to your creative path, you're on your way to the right path.

As mentioned previously, one of the most commonly overlooked tricks to fitting in more is to actually sleep. I also strongly believe in getting an eight-hour night of sleep. Some adults do fine with six, but not me. Lack of sleep is the first drain on my creativity, followed by poor diet and lack of exercise. I also encourage avoiding stress. Financial stress is top of many people's lists. To avoid it, I recommend keeping your day job until your creative endeavor supports you while still finding time for exercise, preparing healthy meals, getting enough sleep, looking after family members, and finding time for your creativity.

Impossible? No.

But I'm not going to lie. It takes discipline, but then so does the work of the creative who pursues their craft full time. It's not easy, but few worthwhile endeavors ever are. Here's how to find much needed time.

CARVING OUT TIME FOR YOUR CREATIVITY

THIS GOES BACK TO OUR GOAL LIST AND ACTION ITEMS. But now, you must also think of them in terms of time spent rather than output.

For instance, let's assume you have a day job, but also creative dreams. That means you can pursue your creative endeavors in the morning before work, during breaks, lunch hour, or after work.

For most people I advise choosing the early morning. This leaves break time to connect with co-workers, lunch time to go to the gym and evening to spend with family or friends as well as take care of other responsibilities I illustrated on my own to-do list such as menu planning, email, studying or even down time.

Let's break it down.

If you're a writer, let's set a goal of working for an hour each morning. Some writers set goals of words written or pages typed, but I think that's too concrete and can lead to a failed mindset. If you decide to put in time and you honestly do so without distractions such as checking email or social media, then you have succeeded.

Decide to put in quality time for your creative endeavor and your imagination will cooperate. Like the stars, you don't always see them, but you know they exist. They may be covered by clouds, but if you spend time looking, you will eventually find them. The same applies to your creativity. Your time may not result in words on the page, but your creative mind showed up for the job and that's half the battle.

A choreographer must show up and put together a series of steps. They must ensure that the movements match the music and that the entire ensemble tells a story and creates a mood. It all starts with just showing up to the studio.

- job
- family
- travel time to and from work
- buying and preparing meals
- volunteering at kids' schools

These are the components of a busy life, but one must prioritize what you want for your future. If the job isn't perfect and you dream of working in a creative field, then you have to put in the time. That means, time in the morning before work, or even a few minutes to jot down ideas during a break. For many people, the evening is often spent watching television. Maybe it's time to give yourself half an hour before your favorite show to visualize the stories that you would create if you worked for a TV network.

Yes, you'll be busy. Yes, it means sacrifice.

Remember, life isn't perfect, but it can be amazing.

20

Creativity Breeds Creativity

I t's not surprising that creative people often have more than one creative outlet.

Jane Seymour is best known for her acting endeavors ("Dr. Quinn Medicine Woman," "Wedding Crashers," "Live and Let Die"), but she has also launched multiple companies and lent her name to various products. She is involved in jewelry design, home furnishing, home decor, and even fine art. With thirteen companies vying for her attention, Jane can't seem to not be creative. Even in her own down time, she often launches into artistic projects with her oil paintings gracing some of her friend's homes and businesses.

Most people see Donald Glover and recognize him from his role on television's "Community," but he is also a writer for "30 Rock", a show runner for "Atlanta", and created the music behind Childish Gambino.

Pierce Brosnan is a fan favorite as James Bond, but when not acting, he paints vibrant and thought-provoking land-scapes and portraits.

Seth Rogan not only acts, but also writes, directs and produces movies.

Highlighting these successful individuals, while meant to inspire, could end up making one feel a bit intimidated. How do they do it? Many people have talent, but these people seem to have an abundance of it. Furthermore, they are privileged to work creatively for a living. It's not luck.

They are accustomed to harnessing their creative energy on command. They are professionals. When the director yells, "action," they get to work. They do the same when they sit quietly and decide to paint or write.

Creativity is within all of us, but for some it's buried deeper. To live a creative and balanced life, we need to learn how to pull that force out from within us and call upon it at a moment's notice. That's where practice and putting the time in makes a difference as well as trusting yourself.

If you recall back to pre-school days, it was easy to be creative. A table covered in paper with crayons beckoned. Pots of paint with brushes tempted us. But now, if we are faced with these art supplies we might let our adult sensibilities lessen our ability to launch into the creative act. Thoughts of self-worth and whether we are good enough influence us. But "good enough" is a matter of opinion. What you must remember is that one person may like realistic drawings, another may be attracted to abstracts.

I had the privilege of watching Piece Brosnan create some of his art. It is shaped by bold colors, free flowing brush strokes and dream-like images of jungles, nature, and even all-seeing eyes. They are mind candy — paintings that inspire conversations, but one wouldn't imagine them in a conservatively decorated home. Creativity and art are as individual as the person creating them. His studio is a place that he can go to and immediately be drawn into his art and I'm sure that process helps him relax and that act makes his creativity flow and become more prolific.

So how can you stir up your own creativity? What if you spend the majority of your day behind a desk? When you have a few moments to be creative, how do you turn on the faucet and let it flow freely? I've got a simple exercise that you can reach for that will turn the clock back to the days when you were a child and creativity came naturally.

Homemade Play-doh! No joke. It's warm and squishy. The act of making it and then playing with it is so satisfying. You can shape it into mini people or baskets, animals or flowers. You don't have to be a world-class sculptor, it's Play-Doh, which means pretty much anything you create will look acceptable. Best part, once you start to manipulate its softness into a form, the creativity bug spreads within you. This is basically the process of giving yourself permission to relax and accept the ideas that naturally brew within your mind.

Then, take those ideas and put them onto paper or canvas or in the dance studio. Creativity breeds creativity. You just need to learn how to launch your creative mindset. It could be getting outdoors for a walk or listening to music that inspires or pumps you up. Once you figure it out, you can call upon your creativity at a moment's notice. Eventually, your creative muse will launch simply because you have entered your creative space, be that a dance studio, painter's loft, or your writer's retreat.

If you have set aside an hour or even half-an-hour each morning to write, you don't want to waste twenty minutes figuring out what to write. You want to sit down and get in your thirty minutes and when the time slot is over, you look at the paper and feel the satisfaction of your productivity.

So look to this recipe for homemade Play-doh. Whip up a batch and sink your fingers into it. Let the memories of childhood wash over you and return to a time when you could approach the art table and jump right in.

Homemade Play-Doh

1 cup flour
1 tablespoon oil
1 teaspoon cream of tartar
1 cup water
1/2 cup salt (This is not a mistake…a half cup!)
food coloring of your choice

Mix ingredients (except food coloring) in a nonstick pan over medium heat until the mixture pulls away from the sides of the pan. Add food coloring and knead until cool and the color is distributed. Keeps three months unrefrigerated.

21

An Argument for
Eavesdropping

R emember when you were little and you hid behind
that big chair in the corner of the living room while
the adults were enjoying a dinner party? Oh wait…that was
me. I had a bad habit of eavesdropping because I found
adults to be fascinating, particularly when they didn't know
a child was listening to their conversations.

Of course, I was caught on more than one occasion and
told never to do it again. I even changed my ways and
obediently left the adult conversation to the adults…until I
became one. Now, I'm going to give you an excuse to eavesdrop like I used to.

Maybe one shouldn't hover at a conspicuous proximity
to perfect strangers, but, is there any harm in tuning your
ears into the conversations of others as they wait for their
drinks at Starbucks? I think not.

In fact, this is precisely the type of conversation that will
make your creativity bloom. Imagine you're writing a scene
involving two teenagers, but maybe you don't have teenagers
living with you or it's been awhile since you were of this
remarkably unselfish age…excuse my sarcasm. I'm told
that's the lowest form of humor, but I couldn't resist.

Every once in awhile forgive yourself the indiscretion of eavesdropping. Instead, allow yourself to use this technique to add authenticity to your writing. I'd even go so far as to encourage you to seek out the character type who you are writing about.

If your story is about an elderly person, perhaps there is a local senior center where you can volunteer your time. If you are writing about a couple in love, get yourself to a movie theater when a rom-com is playing and get in the popcorn line early.

We tend to think of listening in on conversations when the word eavesdrop is mentioned. I also like to think that eavesdropping can be a visual activity. My favorite place for this is the grocery store check-out line. Recently, I spotted a man in his thirties wearing gym attire placing three family-sized portion chicken thighs on the conveyor belt. If that same person had been a woman in her thirties, I would assume the abundance of poultry was for a family with growing teenagers, but considering this guy didn't have a wedding ring, wore a muscle t-shirt and in fact, had ample muscles to spare, I knew it was part of his physical fitness regime.

This could have been material to spark a character study. It's one thing to set out to write a romance about a young guy who is good-looking. However, those are easy traits to imagine. With this insight into what this man bought at the store, I had an idea of how he lives. He's not just a pretty face. It's obvious from looking at him that he's health conscious, but now I knew for sure that this went beyond exercise and extended into his nutrition habits.

Add to that, he was going home to prepare this food. Now, I had a portrait of a man who could whip up a dinner for his date, and what woman wouldn't be impressed with that? I could have followed him out to the parking lot to see if he got into a Mini, a Range Rover, a BMW, or even hopped onto a Harley — each would have given me a new idea and image to develop. But, I feared that action would take me from casual eavesdropper into serious stalker, so I resisted the urge.

If you follow my train of thought, you can consider the idea that eavesdropping is a form of research. Hopefully, that concept will sufficiently ease your guilt on the subject and you will venture forth and become like me, a perpetual eavesdropper in the name of creativity.

Part III

Dispersion - Full Color Spirit

"There are only two days a year when nothing can be done. One is called yesterday and the other is called tomorrow. Today is the right day to love, believe, do and mostly, live." — Dalai Lama XIV

22

Color Outside the Lines

Be Wonderful You!
Malcolm Gladwell perceptively noted that in terms of innovation there are three types of people: innovators, imitators, and all the rest. Upon reading this, it may seem like the first term, innovators, is the only one to strive for, but this isn't necessarily so. Let me explain by leaping ahead and discussing the imitators.

I strive to be upbeat and as such, I prefer a more positive description: trend spotters. Somehow imitators sounds condescending, almost as if we're back in school and being scolded for looking at someone else's paper. Would a creative person strive to be called "an imitator"? It's a trick question because creatives don't simply make innovations and trends. They know how to spot them.

James Andrew Miller, author of "Powerhouse: The Untold Story of Hollywood's Creative Artists Agency," penned this 752 page tomb of a book that details the many agents at this prestigious firm, highlighting not only the many creatives that are represented, but also the agents' ability to spot talent.

Yet, spotting talent isn't as easy as it sounds. The key is

to see the trends before anyone else. Being an innovator is akin to being at the top of the creative food chain, but trend spotting is equally important for creative endeavors. When you spot a trend, your creative brain is already revved up and ready to step on the gas. At a moment's notice, the trend spotter can see an idea or product debut and know exactly how to adapt it for his own purposes and audience. In doing so, he isn't copying; he's providing a product or service that is similar, yet different, to the one in demand in a marketplace not yet saturated.

I would argue that being a trend spotter is a necessary step in becoming an innovator. It's the training wheels taking off on your first two-wheeler adventure. If you aren't innately creative, once you get a feel for spotting trends you're well on your way to being able to create your own. For those who are lucky enough to have active imaginations, the same principles apply. Act on your creative impulses. It's the only time that it's advantageous to leap before looking because you're not investing money, but rather time. But don't forget that time is another commodity. Nobody can buy it regardless of how rich they are.

Whether you act as a trendsetter or jump into a trend the moment you recognize it, do so with your own "Younique" point of view.

In previous chapters I've written about seeing the world with childlike wonder, embracing your instinct to play, and other lessons from pre-school days. (Treating people with kindness, goes without saying!) Now is the time to recall the one pre-school lesson that I encourage you to toss out the window. I refer to coloring inside the lines.

Early childhood educators stress this to see if students can follow directions, act with self-discipline, and manage their time. All important lessons, all necessary for a successful career, but also note that drawing inside the lines is conformity and creatives have permission to set their own rules for design aesthetics.

When children try to draw a face they start off with a Picasso-esque attempt and show it off with pride. But as that same child ages to even ten-years-old, they become aware of realism and want their drawing to reflect what they see in the mirror.

When did they lose their sense of childlike fun or forget to draw just for the sheer enjoyment of it? The example of Picasso's style with his lopsided faces, eyes appearing only on one side, or faces divided into uneven halves is not to imply that a child's work is crude or unrefined. Instead, it shows that our culture deemed something of that nature to not only be worthy, but to be revered in the art world. We should all be so lucky and talented to create such a lopsided face, or perhaps prose that doesn't fit the norm. To create is to take risk.

Creativity is intelligence at play.

23

Habits of Creative, Successful People

Victoria Atkin is an amazing actress and I'm proud to call her a friend. She's worked consistently for over a decade because she is the consummate professional. Her work ethic fits in perfectly to my example of what creative people must do in order to be successful. Simply put, she doesn't only focus on the creative desire; she ensures to nurture the business side as well.

This book has made the case that creativity isn't something that only "right-brain" people possess. Creativity is something that people with a desire to achieve it possess. Yet, once you do achieve a creative status and move toward making your endeavor your primary source of income, you'll need to engage other life skills to keep you afloat. Specifically, you must also nurture your logical side to survive in the business world and take care of your spiritual side in order to be truly successful.

There is no point in being a great painter if you don't know how to run the business of selling your work. Even dancers must attack their art with discipline and know how to communicate effectively, be punctual and in short, act like a professional in order to get the job.

Victoria is a professional actress. To me, that doesn't only mean she makes her living doing what she dreamed of as a child. It also means she acts with professionalism. When you live and work in Los Angeles you have to get used to our horrible traffic. I always assume it takes about an hour to get between appointments in L.A. if you don't live on the Westside. Victoria allows an hour-and-a-half. She gets to every appointment early, giving her time to focus on the meeting, regroup after dealing with the stress of the traffic, locate parking, and overall not walk in at the last minute feeling stressed about walking in at the last minute!

She also shows up prepared. She knows her lines. She knows everyone on set. She doesn't make unreasonable demands or act like a prima donna. She's a grown-up as well as a professional and it shows with every performance.

An Interview with Victoria Atkin

Victoria Atkin is an English actress best known for playing the character Jason Costello, previously known as Jasmine, in the British soap opera "Hollyoaks." Victoria also starred as Evie Frye in the game Assassin's Creed Syndicate. The multi-talented actress proved that creativity is something that expands beyond her acting chops when she penned the romance novel, "London Love."

MW: Try to remember back to the time when you first decided you wanted to be an actress. What was the reaction of your family? How did you convince them to support you?

VA: From a young age, before I could even spell the word 'actress', I knew in my soul this was all I wanted to do. My family were nervous only because they had no experience in the industry. The only way I could convince them to not worry was to prove I could do it. Luckily, my dad was also kind enough to support me with my drama school studies.

MW: Most actors experience having "the door shut" on them when they start out. If this occurred to you, how did you find the strength to carry on?

VA: Of course it happens to all of us in every industry but I began to discover that a rejection is just a redirection.

MW: What characteristics within you make you successful in such a competitive industry?

VA: I am organized and study hard in between jobs. I love to read acting books and watch films and television. A lot of the time it's organizing yourself to get to auditions in plenty of time and being patient - something that is a continuing practice.

MW: How can someone find solace when they are starting out? What advice do you have for weathering the tough times?

VA: Meditate. Spend time in nature and with your family and friends.

MW: Does one have to consider finances when starting out in a competitive field? How does someone balance their dreams with their reality when they are starting out?

VA: Of course, juggling part time jobs you don't want to do in between your acting gigs is a normal practice for the first few years. Like any other industry it's about earning your opportunities through faith, persistence and developing and refining your craft.

I wish success to every single person brave enough to follow their hearts.

24

The Path

After interviewing countless entrepreneurs and creatives, I noticed they had something in common. After doing their initial research or planning, they STOPPED. And then they took action.

The writer must eventually stop outlining.
The dancer must stop stretching.
The painter must stop mixing.
Eventually, you need to just do your art…make your craft.

IT SEEMED AS IF THE DIFFERENCE BETWEEN PEOPLE WHO succeeded and people who failed was as simple as the people who failed often never got started. They stayed in their head and waited for things to be just right.

I thought about this a few years back while my daughter was watching "New Girl" on the television. I loved the theme song with its bouncy tempo and the smooth vocals of its star and producer, Zooey Deschanel. But even more so, I loved the opening two lines: "Hey girl, whatcha doing? Hey girl, where ya going?" It sums up how I hope people will approach their creativity. It's your path to creativity that will set you on a positive course for your entire life.

ENJOY THE JOURNEY AS YOU PURSUE THE DESTINATION.

I WON'T LIE. IT IS INCREDIBLY SATISFYING TO WRITE "THE end" but I've learned to take immense pleasure from letting my thoughts spill onto the page. Sometimes I change my writing method from computer to long-hand. I find that going back and forth gives me a fresh perspective. I love being able to hear the click of the computer keys as my fingers fly over them. It's also great to be just a click away from a Google answer or an online thesaurus, but that can be a distraction as well.

Sometimes I prefer to sit on a bench seat in my kitchen's bay window with a small writing tablet that I can easily hold while enjoying the feel of the sunshine pouring through the window. I find my thoughts flow in a different way when I do this. It comes more from the heart and develops organically.

In contrast, my office is filled with dark wood book-shelves and while it has the appearance of a cozy library, it also is a more formal environment. As such, I find my writing is more focused on facts and plot points than the emotions of the characters. I sit a bit straighter when seated behind my desk with hands poised on my keyboard than I do when in my casual kitchen.

Two locales breed two different styles of writing. Both are necessary for the successful completion of a book, but each one lends itself to a different perspective.

We don't always know where our characters will take us

or how the music will develop. Or even how each brush stroke will guide us. Although I am a big proponent of the need to outline a project, sometimes it takes on a life of its own and veers off course. When this happens, let it guide you.

Dare to follow an unexpected path.

EVEN IF IT LEADS YOUR CHARACTERS, MOVEMENT, OR ART into rocky territory, assume it was meant to go there and now it's your job as an author, dancer, or artist, to find that first seed of inspiration and bring it back on course. Just because your journey — whether on the page or in life — experiences a few rainy patches doesn't mean sunshine isn't in your forecast.

The creative people I've known who have experienced success possessed many of the same key personality traits and work habits. Coincidence? I don't think so. I recognize these traits in successful business executives as well. At the top of the list is…

DESIRE - They have a passionate yearning for their chosen field.

WORK ETHIC - They work tirelessly to accomplish their goals both in terms of time on the job and even before and after their normal work hours.

FOCUS - When they are working, they don't surf the net, get up for coffee breaks, chat on the phone or even fold laundry or clean, if they work at home. They have immense focus for their goal and use their time not just wisely as the adage goes, but frugally as well. They know that time is precious and they guard their own time, always aware that time is a gift.

BELIEVE IN YOURSELF...STEP-BY-STEP TIPS

EMBRACE YOUR FOIBLES.

The phrase that nobody is perfect is not only true, but it's also what makes getting to know people so much fun. Your quirks and idiosyncrasies are what make you unique and memorable.

SELF-BELIEF CAN BE LEARNED.

Think of all the things we can learn later in life from new technology to a dance move. It stems to reason that we can also learn self-belief.

ANALYZE YOUR WEAKNESSES.

Having a weakness is not bad, but ignoring your weaknesses will not help you move forward. Learn how to acknowledge your weaknesses and use them to connect with others. Remember the first point made that nobody is perfect. You might find that you are more relatable to your desired audience because of your weaknesses.

VISUALIZE YOUR BEST POSSIBLE SELF.

Now that you've embraced your foibles, acknowledge your weaknesses. It's time to think of who you want to be. If you were on a speaking tour as a creative artist what message would you want to impart? Start seeing yourself the way you want others to view you.

• • •

TAKE TIME FOR PERKS.

Like an athlete who trains hard and then earns a medal, your journey to success will not be overnight, nor would it feel as sweet if it were that easy. Along the way, you deserve a few perks to sustain your efforts. Be your own cheerleader, your toughest coach, and the voice in your head that says, "You can do this!"

CREATE A VISION BOARD.

It doesn't have to be a work of art, but take time to write down your hopes and dreams. If you don't want to write them, find images that epitomize what you hope to achieve. Pin them up near your work space and admire them often. One day, you're going to pin one of your own glowing reviews.

BELIEVE. YOU WOULDN'T BE READING THIS BOOK IF you didn't believe in your abilities to do something more than what you are living now. You have the desire, the work ethic, the focus. Without self-belief you won't achieve your dreams. This one is a bit trickier because society also tells us not to be egotistical or cocky. And yet, this is perhaps a sexist statement about our society because often times men who possess a bit of cockiness are seen as sexy. In fact, we don't call them cocky. We say they are confident. It's time that women possess that same level of confidence. It doesn't mean you are arrogant. It means you BELIEVE in yourself.

Whether you are a man or woman who believes in their abilities to realize their goals, it doesn't mean that a shred of self-doubt won't creep into your mind from time to time. But with self-belief comes the power to push self-doubt from the forefront of your mind to where it belongs…a passing thought that simply makes you aware of the obstacles and helps you focus your efforts to overcome those difficulties.

AN INTERVIEW WITH SHELLIE BLUM

Shellie Blum was the first female freestyle waterski ramp jumper in the world, but a horrific accident nearly ended her career. Escaping instantaneous death and paralysis from a hangman's broken neck and shattered right jaw, Shellie went on to pen her autobiography and inspire audiences with her tales of perseverance.

MW: You are certainly familiar with set-backs. What driving message within yourself gave you the strength to not only recover, but thrive after your waterskiing accident?

SB: I am actually lucky it happened to me at such a young age, 24. I think this might have been part of the reason I was able to thrive after my accident. I was too young to realize how difficult life was for me at the time. I look back on it, and only now realize how tough things were, but while I was going through it, I just had to keep going.

MW: How do you approach simpler set-backs such as writer's block?

SB: This is going to sound unbelievable, but while I was writing my memoir, I had no writer's block. I wrote it in 25 days. I was like a mad woman possessed. I couldn't think of anything else. I went to sleep thinking about it and woke up thinking about it. Since then, though, I can relate some to writer's block. My solid advice would be to force yourself to write a little bit every day. Bad or good or indifferent, just keep working those mental muscles.

MW: You were one of the first professional, female, freestyle water ski ramp jumpers in the world. It certainly takes dedication to reach that level of expertise. How does that level of commitment find its way into other aspects of your life?

SB: I can be kinda stubborn. Some people that know me and read that will laugh and say, "KINDA?" As I've gotten older I think it's become more important to me that if I say I am going to do something, that I do it. Integrity is a word that comes to mind. I think the world could use more of it. No matter how small or big of a goal it is, you should just keep at it, with whatever level of degree of difficulty you can muster. That way, no one can accuse you of not being successful. You can just tell them, "I'm still working on it."

MW: Are you involved in more than one creative activity now?

SB: To be honest, I can be a little lazy if I don't have a goal in front of me. But when I do, I can be relentless until it's done. I used to pursue an athletic career, and paid little attention to any kind of creative side of me, but since that was abruptly taken away from me, it's taken a long time to fill that hole in my life. I'm glad and lucky I started writing even before my athletic career ended. It was a cathartic way for me to move forward.

My latest creative endeavor is querying Hollywood in hopes of generating interest in a movie about my story. It's a Yea/Boo proposition. Yea! I'm trying to play in the big league media of movies and I think enough of my memoir that it would create good content for a screenplay. Boo! There are days when I think I'm being silly trying to make it happen. But again, there has been something in me from the beginning that refuses to believe that Hollywood won't be able to deny that my story would make a movie. There is some seed or spark of creativity in me that is certain the story should be told cinematically. So I keep querying away. I'm just wondering, if I will have to write the screenplay myself. If so, I will. But I'm not there yet, because I don't feel the same passion for it yet. Not like when I HAD to write my memoir.

MW: Do you think there's a parallel between coming back from an accident such as yours and when creative/artistic people in the public eye must come back after a bad performance or bad review? If so, how?

SB: Sure, how could there not be. When you've had a setback, you can do one of two things: Give up or keep going. One is as likely easy as the other, and I can't be sure how or why some people do one or the other, but I do know that if you keep trying, eventually some of the positives you're striving for will start to manifest themselves in some form or fashion. They may be only teeny tiny little developments, but if you never give up, they will come. And, as I've gotten older, I strive to learn how better to live the moments in between the teeny tiny developments. I guess what I am saying is, "Don't forget to enjoy the journey while trying to reach your goals."

25

Genres of Creativity

Managing expectations fuels your spirit.

In writing, we create a novel within a genre —
romance, thriller, mystery, fantasy, sci-fi. Some books take
the liberty to combine genres or use sub-genres, such as
paranormal romance. But even if you write a book that
balances two genre categories, you must still fulfill reader
expectations.

I think it's important to also keep your own expectations
in check, particularly when launching a new pursuit. If
you're going to go with the genre analogy, you don't want
your expectations to be that of a fantasy novel.

Here's what the fantasy looks like: You imagine spending
your days doing an activity you love. Having evening and
weekends reserved for sheer enjoyment. And best yet, you
reap financial rewards for your effort — enough of a reward
that you no longer have to work your day job.

Once you engage in this pursuit, a different reality sets
in. You no longer dream the fantasy, you live the mystery. As
with any new venture, you don't know what you don't know
until you're face to face with your own limitations. If you're

clever and love research or can network with people who can steer you on the correct course, then it can be a thriller.

There's nothing more exciting than the rush that comes with learning the answer to a problem that plagues you. That is the thriller genre of life, but a creative pursuit doesn't stay in one place long. It evolves and changes, and that is the mystery aspect. You have your creative pursuit but whom you sell it to, the distribution and manufacturing, and the day-to-day business issues remain a mystery until solved.

Just as there are many genres of books, your creative pursuits will move through different genres. If you have a creative inspiration, you will also experience the romance genre. You work for the love of your craft. Your love has to be unwavering because this will keep you going through every other "genre" of your creative distinction.

Navigating these genres of creativity is a learning experience, one that continues and evolves as you do.

BE A LIFELONG LEARNER

I OFTEN ASK WRITERS WHO TAKE MY CLASSES WHAT they're currently reading. It's a bit of a trick question, and for that, I apologize. Inevitably, one of them says they don't have time to read. I strongly believe that you must be a reader in order to be a writer.

I'm sure there are exceptions…people who are prodigies and have an innate instinct for their craft. I recently heard about a six-year-old who listened to a piece of classical music in school and after hearing it for a week, she went over to the piano and played the melody by ear. However, do you know what the teacher did immediately? She went to the phone and called the parents telling them that they had to get their daughter professional music lessons.

Why? The daughter was obviously gifted on her own. She had a natural talent without studying others. But, her teacher knew that additional lessons could take her from good to great. We can always learn and improve. Whether in a formal or informal setting, you should study things that interest you and seek out people who have knowledge to share.

I believe that I'm a great editor. I can take an author's work and rid it of repetitive language and get to the heart of their story. I can see the whole picture even when it isn't laid out in the best light. I can restructure a story so that the characters are compelling and the plot is riveting. And yet, I know that there are people out there who can teach me a few lessons.

Bryan Cohen, who has graciously contributed to this book, has a tremendous course on book marketing, which I have taken, learned from and applied the lessons. To go back to my rainbow analogy, we are each small beams of light in this big world of reflected images. It doesn't serve us well to carry ego or arrogance that we have nothing more to learn.

We all need self-belief, but that is very different from arrogance.

26

Inspiration on a Vacation

When he took his "small step" onto the moon's surface in 1969, Neil Armstrong spoke the phrase that would become one of history's most famous one-liners. Every small accomplishment in your creative endeavor, be it a newly conceived chapter or even one line is "one small step" in your greater pursuit.

But the "what-ifs" that I wrote about in the earlier portion of this book are not just seeds of doubt that plague your mind, they affect your spirit too. Read on to find out how we're going to vanquish those unnecessary and unworthy thoughts.

First, you need to analyze if you're truly in a slump. It's probably a matter of seeing the cup being half-full. Let me explain. A non-creative day is inevitable, but the way you approach these slumps is what sets apart the professional from the hobbyist.

Remember, you are moving toward turning your creative goals into a business, which means approaching your time wisely. Don't underestimate the value in spending daily time with your creative endeavor. The creative "muscle" needs daily exercise.

Earlier, I provided some specific writing prompts to help with this task. Below are some sites that regularly update their writing prompts. Take a few minutes to see if one of these fits your personality.

Remember, it doesn't matter if you write a passage for your current project, dutifully following one chapter and then the next. Your goal is simply to create regularly. The more you create, the more chances that something will stick and will become your next great project. If not, maybe it will spark your next big idea. Approach your creativity as a life long endeavor.

WRITING PROMPT SITES:

STORYADAY.ORG
http://storyaday.org/category/inspiration/writing-prompts/
Each prompt is intentionally ambiguous, adaptable to any genre and style, and comes with a list of tips to help you delve deeper into the ideas.

DIYMFA WRITER IGNITER
http://diymfa.com/writer-igniter
Simply hit a button and take a whirl! Writer Igniter generates a situation with a character, prop and setting.

WRITING PROMPTS THAT DON'T SUCK
http://awesomewritingprompts.tumblr.com/
The name says it all. There are over 600 writing prompts, mostly one-liners and snippets of dialogue and word lists.

. . .

TUMBLR

https://www.tumblr.com/tagged/writing-prompts

Tumblr has a strong writing community. Simply use the hashtag #writingprompt to find a list.

WRITERS' DIGEST WRITING PROMPTS

http://www.writersdigest.com/prompts

Writer's Digest is a great resource for many writing questions, not just prompts.

REDDIT WRITING PROMPTS SubREDDIT

https://www.reddit.com/r/WritingPrompts/

Reddit tends to showcase writing that is inspired by today's news. The prompts are user-submitted and often in the genres of apocalyptic/sci-fi/fantasy/horror topics.

YOU'LL QUICKLY FIND HOW EFFECTIVE THESE PROMPTS are for getting your brain into full speed ahead mode. It's like the warm-up to your work-out, but that doesn't mean you have to stop and switch into your current project.

If you're on a roll, keep going. Just because you've fulfilled the requirements of the prompt doesn't mean you should put on the brakes if the ideas continue to flow.

I was once tasked with writing a short story to be added to an anthology. I had an idea and started writing. I knew the maximum word count they would accept and I actually wondered how difficult it would be to get to the required 5,000-7,500 words. I had written novels of up to 70,000 words so my fear wasn't a matter of if I could write extensively, but rather if my idea for a relatively simple short story would amount to that number of words.

I quickly found my writing rhythm. Ideas poured out of me and the story expanded beyond my original idea. It was one of those magical moments of creativity when everything just clicked. But then I was faced with a problem I never anticipated. The maximum word count was fast approaching and I hadn't completed my story. I still had thoughts to write and ideas to share. There were scenes evolving in my mind that I had yet to put down on paper. Should I put everything to a sudden halt and wind things down in a brusque approach to "the end"? Absolutely not.

If the creative muse has graced you with her presence, do not send her packing. My short story ended up becoming a novella that sparked an entire series. It was far too long to submit to the anthology, but it made more sense to **let the story take on wings and fly**. I knew that I needed to create an entirely different short story for the anthology. But, having experienced this rush of creativity gave me the confidence to know that I would be able to do just that.

It was the best possible ending -- two stories born out of one experience.

27

Your Creative Raison d'Etre

How do you feel when you take part in your creative activity? Sitting down to write if you're a writer should be pleasurable. It shouldn't be viewed like a high school English class assignment (no offense to high school English teachers). But I say this because you are creating your story filled with your characters and their problems as well as their hopes and dreams. It's your idea!

Similarly, if you're a dancer, every time you go into the studio it should fill you with a sense of home. It's where you feel safe, comfortable and are given a sense of empowerment and discovery.

If your creative endeavors don't make you happy -- if you aren't looking forward to the time you've carved out each day to work on them -- then perhaps you need to evaluate *why* you want to pursue this goal.

LET'S THROW OUT SOME WORDS THAT MAY DESCRIBE SOME people's reasons for pursuing creative dreams:

Happiness vs Recognition

Satisfaction vs Applause

Enjoyment vs Fame

Raison d'etre vs Money

All of these are reasonable ideals of why we pursue our creative side, but only the left hand column are good reasons. The list on the right may come if you pursue your craft with dedication. They will come if you keep your creativity fresh and never rest on your laurels. And, if you can find an audience that connects with your material.

But it is the last item on the left — your creative raison d'être — your reason to be — that should drive you the hardest. You can't imagine not pursuing creativity in your life. Your creative side lies within your very core and to not wake up each day and do it would make for an unsatisfying life.

Your creative dreams will not be realized because of money or fame or even the validation of finding an audience. Your dreams are realized within yourself. Similarly, they become reality when you appreciate and recognize that they are an innate part of you.

You live your dream when you make that conscious decision to practice that which satisfies you.

- If you are a writer, you write.
- If you are a dancer, then you must dance.
- Make music if you are a musician.
- Paint and sculpt if you are an artist.
- Build your project if you are an artisan.

Each of these creatives becomes successful by doing… and the moment they step into their creative world, the sun shines just a bit brighter for each.

28

Act with Kindness

I find that writers who write for the love of the craft rather than a hope of making money tend to produce better results. They aren't chasing trends and trying to replicate the latest best seller or blockbuster movie. Let me share an example that exemplifies this theory.

When I first started in the entertainment industry I worked as a publicist. Many of my accounts were non-profits who had celebrity support, and I also repped those celebs. My job was to promote the non-profit first and foremost, but often times, it was the celebrity attached to the organization that attracted the media.

The fact that they weren't doing something to benefit themselves, but rather, because they believed in the greater good was evident and the media would flock to the events. Yes, the resulting media storms also benefitted the celebrity, but it was evident that by doing good, they felt good.

WORK FOR A CAUSE, NOT APPLAUSE

• • •

This is where a love of the cause, rather than chasing applause is the way to go.

The media would naturally mention the celebrity attachment, but their names gained valuable publicity because they were associated with something more noble than promoting themselves or their latest work. By doing something good for others, they were doing good for themselves.

You might say that you're not famous so this advice doesn't apply to your life and it certainly won't help to further your creative career. This couldn't be farther from the truth. Let me explain with examples from the indie author world.

When I first met author Lizzy Ford I asked how she seemed to have such a strong connection to her readers when she only "speaks" to them via Facebook. I was a bit old school at the time and still felt that the personal connection, a face-to-face, was needed in order to make a connection.

While it's amazing to meet someone in person, I was wrong about this being a necessity. Lizzy acts with such generosity, giving her knowledge and time to strangers… who then become virtual friends and followers. As one of her Facebook friends told me, "Lizzy could write the phone book and I would read it."

So I tried it. I started to offer books to people just because. I commented on their posts and offered help to their problems. Soon…in fact, very soon, I was blessed with new friends who returned the favors of kindness.

Now, I have an amazing personal assistant, Jessica Molina Ramirez, who I met on FB. I live in California; she lives in Texas, but it's as if she's in my office as we check in regularly and I wake up to find that she's already been busy with my social media.

The same applies to Tracy Ehlers, who lives all the way

in Australia. If it weren't for Tracy, Mia Fox, my pen name would not be splattered across so many reader groups.

Be supportive when people post about their problems or highlight their triumphs. Commenting on Facebook or Twitter or Snapchat is starting a conversation. These people have showed me incredible kindness and in turn, I offer them the first reads of my books. Best of all, I feel I know them even though we are states and sometimes continents apart.

AN INTERVIEW WITH KM WEILAND

KM Weiland is the IPPY, NIEA, and Lyra Award-winning and internationally published author of the Amazon bestsellers "Outlining Your Novel" and "Structuring Your Novel," as well as "Jane Eyre: The Writer's Digest Annotated Classic", the western "A Man Called Outlaw," the medieval epic "Behold the Dawn," the portal fantasy "Dreamlander," and the historical/dieselpunk adventure "Storming." When she's not making things up, she's busy mentoring other authors on her award-winning blog, Helping Writers Become Authors.

MW: There's a phrase, "Work for a cause, not applause." You write historical fiction, but some people might know you from your vast articles on writing techniques. Why is it important to you to give back to the writing community?

KMW: Something I've always tried to focus on in inviting others to learn from me is putting my service to them at the forefront. I try very hard never to take people for granted. When they visit my site or buy my books, they're doing me as much of a kindness as I am them, and I try to always keep that front and center. I'm only able to do what I do because of the kind and generous writers I'm blessed to interact with every day.

MW: Would you rather be remembered for your author mentorship or your books?

KMW: I'd be happy to be remembered for either. Or rather, it's not as important to me be remembered as a person as it is that my work continues to have a positive ripple effect in people's lives. My fiction is certainly more important to me, so if it was up to me to choose which would have the larger impact, that would be my choice. But who am I to say? I wish for whichever has the ability to make the largest positive impact to be remembered for the longest time.

MW: You turn out a large number of blog posts each year. Can you share a secret of your productivity or perhaps your personal writing schedule?

KMW: I like to say, in all seriousness, that schedules are my secret weapon. I manage my time strictly and I'm always tweaking my daily schedule to try to get my best productivity while still balancing the need for relaxation and recharging.

I like to get my writing done first thing in the morning, while the day is still fresh. Right now, I'm experimenting with staving off email and Internet activities until the very last thing in the work day. Blogging gets its own day, in which I take care of all the weekly blogging duties in one fell swoop.

Minimizing distractions is key, so I'm very strict with myself about wasting time on the Internet, watching videos, or even reading news sites.

MW: How do you view the concept of creativity when you are also so involved in the business of writing?

KMW: It's something I'm very aware of. First and foremost, I make a point of embracing the joy of writing—embracing the quirkiness, the adventure, even the uncertainty. Art of any kind isn't worth pursuing without passion. So I try to always remember why I'm writing. I cherish my passion, and nurture it. I write every day, and I joke that I guard my desk with a machete and flamethrower! Writing time is sacred, and I learned early on that if I didn't respect that, I would never get anybody else to.

MW: Any words of advice about reviews (and bad ones) for writers?

KMW: Whenever you're down about a bad review, jump on Amazon, look up your favorite novel by someone else, and take a look at the one-star reviews. Instant perspective!

29

Who Are You?

Create Your Personality —
When we think of people we like or more aptly the characteristics of likable people, we don't necessarily note their I.Q. or ability to recite the periodic table or knowledge of astrophysics or world history. Sure, those things might make someone interesting, but you engage in interesting and stimulating conversation simply by being well read and staying up to date on current news affairs.

What makes a person likable are personality traits such as kindness, generosity, compassion, empathy, and friendliness. The best part about these traits is that they can be launched into immediately. You learned this stuff in preschool.

Humans are innately social creatures. It's in our DNA. It's even in the Bible. We meet people. We build relationships. It actually takes more energy to be an asshole than it does to be kind. True, the assholes of the world exist. They may even have their own meet-ups, but if you come into contact with them try this: listen.

More often than not, angry people just want to vent. Be kind. Offer an ear, but also be cognizant of your own time because it's valuable. But I bet you will turn that person around and the asshole club will have one less member. Your reward will be that you feel pride in making someone happy. The act of being friendly is not a strategic one with the person who shows kindness first being labeled weaker or desperate. Rather, place yourself in the role of teacher and show them how to do it.

DON'T FIND YOURSELF...CREATE YOURSELF.

WE OFTEN HEAR PEOPLE COMMENT THAT THEY WANT "TO find themselves." I would argue that they know exactly who they are, but they aren't able to live the life they visualize. Do you find yourself in this situation? Let's analyze potential reasons.

The first is responsibility. Starting out, a creative job might not earn you as much as your current job. This is when I say that you have to be a grown up first. Perhaps you have a family, a mortgage, student loans, maybe a car payment. Whatever your financial responsibilities, it's not a good idea to throw away a steady job in favor of one that might be more fun, but isn't as high paying. But that doesn't mean it won't become high earning.

Rewards don't happen overnight, but neither do opportunities. This is when desire and passion for your creative endeavor must be harnessed and then unleashed. If you have the desire to enter a competitive field, but your passion will be unfulfilled if you never try, then that's your answer. You have to go for it, but when you do, it means realizing that you approach your passion like a grown-up. You work hard at it.

Cathy Braffet Richardson worked as art director at

Disney. On the surface, it seemed like she had the perfect job for someone like herself who dreamed of being an artist. But the trouble was that although she worked in art, she wasn't allowed to let her creative instincts take off. She had to mimic the art of her superiors. It left her frustrated because she had her own style of art that she desperately wanted to pursue.

Yet, she also had to pay her rent. So every night after putting in a ten hour day (this is the entertainment industry we're talking about), she would go home, grab a bite, and then sit down at her drafting table and stay there until it was time for sleep. No television. No movies. No mid-week outings. Just the pursuit of her creative dream. She did this on average of five out of seven nights, as if it were a second job. Why?

Because to not do so was unfathomable to Cathy. Drawing was her way to wind down before bed much in the way television is for others. She couldn't imagine not doing it. More importantly, she knew that to get the life she wanted, she needed to put in the time.

She knew that there was a sequence to her life and it was time for her to focus on her job in order to keep it and pay the rent, but also the future job she envisioned. It paid off. She now has created her own brand, her own company, and her former employer, Disney, is one of her clients along with many other prestigious companies.

She says she is living the life she always dreamed. It took a few years. It took hours of hard work. Most importantly, it took a mindset of belief in herself mixed with a healthy dose of realistic living. She was a grown up and took care of her responsibilities, pursued her craft by carving out solid work time each day, and persevered until it paid off.

An Interview with Cathy Brafffet Richardson

Cathy Brafffet Richardson is an illustrator and designer who began at the Walt Disney Company and now has her own design business where she creates visual experiences for some of the most recognizable brands in the marketplace, with companies spanning from the entertainment and retail industry to the private sector.

MW: What comes to mind when I ask you to describe how you approach creativity?

CR: I think if you are passionate about something, like Nike figured out, "Just Do It." I know it's never that easy, but I'm learning that for me, having an intension and a passion for what you love to do is half the battle.

As I continue to age, I look back at my priorities, and who was in my life at that time of starting my business. Now, as a mom of three, it's funny how my passions have shifted, but I always have gratitude for who I was and where I was at that time in my life and how creating Cathy B Design twenty years ago has shaped my life as it is now.

Cathy B Design is my fourth child (not including my husband and my dog). I've obsessed over it, feared for it, rejoiced with it, I've bent backwards for it, I lay awake many nights about it and as my child, "we" never close down. It's a 24-7 commitment. This "relationship" has had its ups and downs with my "self", family and my marriage. We have all been tested and challenged by it, grown closer because of it, and have truly enjoyed the benefits and graces of Cathy B Design.

My goals for my business have changed dramatically from the days in my little Pasadena, California apartment while I moonlighted on projects after working my day job. As my focus and dreams shifted with age, so have experiences and life's changes also shaped me.

MW: While working at Disney, how did you find the energy to go home after a long day and pursue your art?

CR: Energy is your soul's passion; it was something that I felt I needed to do. It not only thrilled me to try this (at 25 years old) but also being so young, I was not too worried about failing. Gosh, I wish Pinterest existed back then!

MW: How did you balance your earlier career with your dream/pursuit of your own business?

CR: I do thank God for giving me this focus and intension for starting this business. Sleepless nights in my 20s were a big part of the plan back then and they still are at 47! That and a great boyfriend who tried very hard to accept the nights I could not go to a party/dinner/plans and supported my dreams. I ended up marrying him, so that all worked out great. Business building 101 for me has always been to have gratitude for those around you and let them know it.

MW: How do you continue to manage family responsibilities with running a business?

The business has changed; the expectations have changed. It's still a struggle with family and work, but I am so grateful for what I do along with the people I work for and with. The biggest thing now is starting to understand that I am NOT in control. I can not worry about the quiet months and can not freak out with the busy months. To stay focused with intention is my mantra. Fame and fortune are at the bottom of the barrel these days, but the inspiration to others is on the top. Volunteer work, teaching my daughter my craft and working with people I respect are my top priorities with Cathy B Design.

MW: What advice do you have for people who want to pursue a creative endeavor but can't afford to give up their "day job."

CR: Just DO IT! No excuses. Place it on the priority scale, pray for it and believe in yourself. Make it happen. Set baby goals, and even then, don't beat yourself up if you fail and something gets in the way. We are not always in control of our destiny, but I believe there is a plan.

I tell my kids all the time, give it 110% and whatever happens is what was meant to be...and that will be good enough. Whether your dream is to be like Martha Stewart, open a shop, inspire others, or share your gifts...if this in your heart, it will shine.

ON THE FLIP SIDE OF CATHY'S RESPONSIBLE PERSONAL AND professional journey comes a screenwriter I used to know. He so desperately wanted to be in Hollywood that he left the security of his day job. His reason, he explained, was that he wanted to devote more time to his chosen career -- that of a screenwriter. He was working a rather boring job at the time in an office.

I understand that desire. I also understand his claim that after a day at his boring job, he would come home feeling drained and uninspired to write. What I don't understand were the numerous wrong choices he made in spite of getting advice to the contrary.

He believed his time would be best spent networking with agents and producers. The trouble he learned is that these professionals are most interested in individuals who have a body of work, not just one script.

Instead of spending time writing the next script while waiting for the first one to sell, he decided to stop all creative endeavors to peddle his script in the hope of an easy sale. Making matters worse, to free up his time to do this, he quit his job and tried to make money via day trading of stocks, which is an extremely risky endeavor in which someone buys and sells by the hour, watching risky stocks rise and fall.

The way he attacked his dream made no sense. He quit his job to pursue screenwriting, but rather than write, he spent time trying to meet with movers and shakers who wouldn't meet him because he wasn't writing and what free time he had was spent fretting over declining stock prices. Had he stuck to his day job, regardless of whether it was boring, and written in the early morning, during lunch hours and at night, it would have probably paid off. Think about it like this, if he wrote only one page a day, he would have a script's first draft complete in around three months.

Instead, he found it difficult to get back into the writing groove because he was so rusty at accessing that part of his brain. The irony of his situation was apparent to everyone from the outside except for him.

He claimed his boring job was not conducive to being creative. Yet money challenges that come from not having a job and day trading, coupled with a lack of a diligent time put into his creative pursuit left him financially broke and creatively broken. His writing muscle had completely atrophied.

HOW TO BE A GROWN-UP

1. Carve out time for your creative endeavors outside of your day job.
2. Don't quit your day job!
3. Maintain childlike dreams and wonder.
4. Live responsibly.
5. Realize that there aren't any get rich quick schemes.
6. Be an innovator.
7. Surround yourself with positive influences.

30

Spiritual Connectedness

Being creative often starts simply by being more aware. Be aware of your creative possibilities. Inspiration isn't a gift that some receive and others don't like a tap on the shoulder from a helpful muse or angel. It comes from within you. You will find inspiration from this book in the sense that I hope to instill in you a sense of self-belief.

You can do this!

(Go on…highlight that right now!) You have a dream and you're going to go for it.

And once you decide to go for it, your mind will be open to more ideas and your physical self will be more accepting to putting in the time it takes to accomplish your goals.

Don't be afraid to start for fear of failure. The only thing you should fear is being sedentary, not just in the physical sense because getting up and moving gets the creative juices flowing, but also mentally…spiritually.

Having a sedentary mind means not daring to dream, not being willing to take risks that are scary in order to create the life you want. Playing it safe is not always equivalent to responsibility. Sometimes the most responsible thing you can do is simply to try.

***

Cultivate Creativity

- Try to learn something new.
- Try to develop a plan for your creative venture.
- Try to put yourself out there and let others know about your dreams.

The only way you can let yourself down is by not trying.

And regarding that, a quick word about reviews. I could have easily included this thought into the chapter about expectations as we have expectations (or hopes) of good reviews on the work we do. But I chose to put it here in the section that relates to our sprit because the occasional bad review can be so disheartening to our psyche.

But one can't let a bad review take away your love of the creative endeavor. Remember the phrase, "What doesn't kill us only makes us stronger." This must have applied to an author reading their first bad review. To remain positive is key to your success. That doesn't mean you don't reevaluate yourself from time to time, making changes where deemed necessary.

Bad reviews can be looked upon as helpfulness disguised for Halloween. Some people aren't diplomatic and that can hurt. Look past the hurt or the costumed grim reaper and realize that a bad review is not the death of your career. It is an opportunity for reinvention.

***

Positivity

. . .

I READ A STUDY THAT STATED "SADNESS INHIBITS NEW ideas." Thinking back to times when positivity escaped me and a peek outdoors seemed to reveal more grey than sunny skies, I thought the results of this study were oversimplified (might I even add, I rolled my eyes and said 'duh'). Of course we have more ideas when we're happy. You don't need a scientific study to tell you that. But, what you do need are concrete methods for how to rid yourself of the doldrums when they strike.

After polling my amazing Facebook followers and reflecting on my own experiences, I've compiled this go-to list that's sure to brighten your mood on a less than stellar day.

- curl up with a good book
- watch a sit-com (even an old repeated one does the trick)
- watch your favorite movie (same as above — I can watch Bridget Jones' Diary umpteen times and it never gets old)
- ice cream (any flavor, any time as long as it's in moderation)
- walk the dog
- visit or phone a friend
- cook a complete dinner (and relish in your accomplishment)
- exercise

In India, they have groups that gather for laughter clubs. During these meetings, the group will break out into laughter. At first it's forced, but soon the laughter becomes contagious and seeing the person next to you laugh invokes the same reaction in yourself until it's a real honest and loud guffaw.

It might not seem completely natural to stand up, open

your mouth and start laughing, but why not try it? The point of the exercise is that it's hard to be sad when you're laughing. You may not break into a hysterical, side-aching fit, but that's not really the goal. Let's recall how we got onto this subject…sadness is a creativity killer. By attempting laughter you will naturally boost your mood at least a small amount.

Karen Gasper, Ph.D. and social psychology professor at Penn State University, authored a study that supported the theory that creativity is boosted by happiness. She found that people in happy moods are found to be better at solving problems, word associations, and generating story endings, all which are imperative for writers.

One can't always force happiness. Life happens and sometimes it's not all roses and kittens. However, you can make a conscious decision to strive for happiness and work towards fulfillment.

31

Finding Fulfillment

Part of creating a Full Color Life is knowing what areas of your life need the most attention in order to give you the most fulfillment. This is not about being selfish and doing what you want. It's about learning how to focus your energies for maximum results.

In my quest to lead a balanced life, I must assess what's most important to me. Here's my top three: Raising children who are able to go out into the world and contribute to society and act with kindness. Maintaining strong relationships with my spouse, family and friends. Working in a field that I'm passionate about. These quests contribute to my overall happiness. Write down your top three now.

Why is this important? When we are happy, we have the mental energy to dream up creative ideas that will bring fulfillment to our lives. You must also take the time to consider if the reality of your dreams matches your expectations.

One must be comfortable in their creative mind. What I mean by this is that some artists find it lonely in there. The solitude can be overwhelming. Some creatives stop the pursuit of the life they imagined because of this, but it doesn't have to be this way. Your life as a creative doesn't have to be solitary. You can network with others. You can do research that brings you out into the world.

Want to write a detective novel? Make an appointment at your local police station and come prepared with a short list of questions. Want to write a musical score? Spend time in a dancer's studio to gain inspiration about their movement. You are creative and gifted with a viable imagination. The possibilities are endless.

But inevitably you need that quiet time and you need to learn to enjoy it and be productive in it. Remember...you want a creative life. But like anything, it has ups and downs. Learn to enjoy both.

One way to get used to the solitude is with simple meditation. I'm not talking about going on a spiritual retreat where you sit in silence for an entire weekend. I'm talking baby steps such as lying in savanna or "dead body" pose.

In this yoga pose, one lies down and fixates their eyes on one spot on the ceiling. Your goal is to not only lie completely still, but to also clear your thoughts of absolutely everything. Try this for just two minutes. That's just 120 seconds. Then, see if your mind isn't more prepared for the hard work of sitting in front of your computer, ready to create.

The idea is that by learning to rid your mind of all ideas and thought, you will be ready for the influx of fresh, new ones that are ready to infiltrate your sub-conscious. Most importantly, it will help you to not only be used to quiet, but to relish it.

Most of us aren't ever alone in the quiet. We turn on the television or music, text or call a friend, view Snapchat or Instagram. The problem with so much stimulation is that when it's time to just be alone with our ideas, they aren't present. I mean this in both the yoga term of "being present," meaning to be fully aware of what you are doing at that given moment, as well as being ready to sit down and do the job you've set out to accomplish.

This is your dream. Don't let it be fleeting or come to you in sleep. Live it. Nurture it.

32

Enjoy the Journey

I ronically, creative endeavors are often results focused. The writer works to get to the end of his novel. The same is true for the songwriter or composer. We aim to finish. Often the people we're surrounded with contribute to this mindset with friendly albeit less than helpful inquiries such as, "How's the book coming along?" That innocent conversation starter can spur a myriad of negative thoughts.

My suggestion: Smile and nod. Truth is, that book doesn't just "come along" like a promptly scheduled train. Some days may be slow moving with inspiration and ideas seemingly on vacation. Or you may be thinking that you've written mountains of work of which a very small percentage will actually be found in the final draft. Filmmakers, especially documentarians, know this quite well as often times hours of footage ends up on the cutting room floor.

Filmmakers can relate to the feeling that the race to the finish is a long one, but unlike other creatives, they don't fret over that innocent inquiry about progress. They have embraced the journey of their creative trip. They look at small accomplishments without worry that the final product isn't anywhere near completion. Their answer would simply be a factual statement -- they're still researching, still looking for sources -- still interviewing the sources they've found.

James Cameron, director of "Titanic" and many other films, is known for being a visionary but also so dedicated to his craft that those working with him may find his diligent pursuit overwhelming. Yet he knows that in order to be proud of a project, you don't rush it.

In an interview with the Academy of Achievement, he said, "What people call obsession or passion, for me is just a work ethic. Have I thought of everything? Have I thought of every detail? Is this the best the scene can be? It comes from a healthy insecurity that makes you better as an artist."

In short, the project is done when it's done.

When faced with that inevitable question of how's your project going, stop for a moment and take pride in what you have accomplished. There's nobody competing neck and neck with you. You may have competition in your field, but there is room for many to climb to the top. The truth is, the public is fickle. Consumers will place someone at the top of the heap, but they want to admire many.

Accomplishments in terms of writing a book doesn't mean writing "the end" on the page. Imagining a scene and how it unfolds is a writing accomplishment. Describing the nuances of a character's appearance will add depth to your writing. The plot twists and turns will keep the reader engaged. These are your personal accomplishments every time you create.

It's not about the individual writing session as you won't necessarily know every plot point the moment you get your idea for your novel, but for each idea that does strike, take pride in it. When someone asks about your writing, don't say it's hard or you're stuck. Negative thoughts only breed more negativity. Instead, say something like, "Great! I just figured out where my character is headed and what they desire."

Even if you have to add, "at least in this scene" at the end of that sentence.

This mindset will change the direction of the conversation from someone giving you a pity pat on the back to a high five. Your novel is a journey and you need faith and self-belief that the road will take you to completion.

33

A Case for Creativity

The link between creativity and improved mental, physical, and spiritual health is well established.

Our future as a people depends on creativity. U.S. schools are more focused on core subjects, spending hours of training in order to boost standardized test scores. Children experience more stress than ever before. As parents and concerned citizens, we need to see the correlation between creativity and an improved life, and fight for the arts to be taught in our schools.

Experts agree that when we work creatively and with a passion for a project, we are physiologically able to work longer with less stress. That certainly equates to a much healthier and productive way of competing in a world market.

Children and teens don't have the same creative hang-ups that adults carry. Give children a tub of paint, a brush, and some paper and they will create without hesitation. Today's teens and twenty-somethings have grown up in a YouTube culture where Justin Bieber had the confidence to post videos of himself singing.

Music manager Scooter Braun's discovery of Bieber and

the pop idol's subsequent rise to super stardom launched a movement among young people and the idea that it's acceptable to put yourself out there. Do they have a fear of failure? Some might, but in today's media hungry world, even failed attempts can bounce back and reinvent themselves.

Whether you like or dislike our "look at me" culture, the act of being creative benefits everyone. What this means is that we have a responsibility to promote creativity in schools so that young people grow up with the sense that being innovative is something to strive for — something that can potentially make our world flourish.

We also must encourage older generations to awaken their dormant creativity. We were all children once, squeezing Play-Doh, sliding pudgy hands through wet paint, stacking blocks to form our idea of the perfect structure. The instincts toward creativity haven't gone away; they've just gone to sleep.

To jumpstart our creativity is to not only live a happier life, but a healthier one as well. There are definitive links between creativity and better physical and mental health. People who take part in creative endeavors have been found to be happier and less stressed with fewer incidents of depression. These health benefits make us more resilient to illness as well as able to better manage our weight and glucose levels. Other physical health benefits include fewer upper-respiratory infections and cardiovascular disease.

Creative people are proven to be better problem-solvers, have longer lasting relationships, and better inter-personal skills.

Confucius once said that if you choose a job you love, you will never work a day in your life.

Conclusion

Follow the Rainbow —

Regardless of how desirable it is to live a creative life, it's not a pursuit that comes to fruition overnight. If it were that easy, every book published would hit the best-seller list. Every dancer would find themselves on Broadway. Every aspiring chef would earn a Cordon Blue award. It's not easy, but you've taken the first steps toward success.

Might I add, the same first steps that every award-winning person at the top of your field of choice also took when they were starting out. The good news is that in spite of not being an easy pursuit, your steps are very straightforward.

Desire + Perseverance = Completion of Your Goal

You get an idea, both about what you want from your life and how you're going to pursue it.

And then, never stop.

Never.

Yes, you act responsibly and behave like a grown up by

taking care of yourself and family first. But then you analyze your time and how to carve out more of it and in that time, you work like a demon until the project is finished.

Only then do you get a well-deserved pat on the back and a big spoonful of pride. You've come a long way, but you stayed on course until you crossed the finish line. Your job isn't over as you probably need to revise your work and then market it. But with the heavy lifting being complete, a wonderful epiphany should occur to you...if you finished this first project, you can do it again, which is how a career is born.

The first novel is the hardest. You don't know if you'll ever complete it. The same is true for writing your first piece of music, choreographing your first dance or any of the multitude of other creative endeavors. But now you know how it's done...you are a creative! It's part of you and nobody can take that away.

I hope that with this new knowledge you have also found a greater sense of self-worth and pride. We have only one life to live. Why not make it rainbow colored and full of creative energy?

Acknowledgments

I am blessed to have had support from a long list of individuals.

To the fabulously creative "creatives" who granted me interviews: *Victoria Atkin, Shellie Blum, Bryan Cohen, Lisa Douthit, Marie Ferro, Tracey Noonan, Cathy Richardson*, and *KM Weiland*. You are all an inspiration to me and I feel so privileged to know all of you.

To *Rachel Thompson* for her continued support and mentorship that turned into a wonderful friendship. Thank you for your guidance and Nutella recipes.

To *Melissa Flickinger*…thank you for helping to spread the word about the benefits of a Full Color Life.

I'm always blown away at the kindness of strangers. I do believe that the world is inherently good and *Gwynnith Smith* you have proved that to me again. You read this book in its early draft and made it better just because you were asked. Thank you.

To **Barb Drozdowich**, I can see how the apple doesn't fall far from the tree in your family. I know where you got your generosity and I can't seem to go even a week without contacting you. I think the world of you!

And finally, to my family…I love you all so much.

Bibliography

fastcompany.com, April 17, 2012, "The Science of Creativity" by Tina Seelig.

fastcompany.com, December 3, 2013, "The Science Of Great Ideas—How to Train Your Creative Brain" by Belle Beth Cooper.

fortune.com, December 1, 2004, "The New Science of Naming" by Alex Frankel.

greatist.com, November 5, 2013, "The Scientific Reasons Why Being Creative Can Make You Happier" by Shana Lebowitz.

Harvard Business Review, October 17, 2014, "What You Eat Affects Your Productivity" by Ron Friedman.

helpguide.org, "The Benefits of Play for Adults".

inc.com, October 9, 2015, "Want to Be More Creative? Get Used to Embarrassing Yourself" by Ilan Mochari.

psychologytoday.com, May 7, 2012, "The Right Questions Can Increase Life Satisfaction" by Leslie Becker-Phelps Ph.D. Leslie Becker-Phelps Ph.D.

self.com, April 19, 2015, "Rosie Hungtington-Whiteley: Sailing Through Her Life and Loving It" by Laurie Sandell.

self.com, May 17, 2015, "SELF-Made Women Who Inspire: Lyndsay Cruz" by Devin Tomb.

Tharp, Twyla, The Creative Habit, Simon & Schuster, 2003.

telegraph.co.uk, December, 3, 2013, "Lacking inspiration? Exercise Found to Boost Creativity" by Sarah Knapton.

About the Author

Mia Walshaw is the principal of Evatopia, a creative agency catering to writers with divisions supporting publishing and marketing. Additionally, she works as an editor and book packager serving both independent writers as well as major publishing houses.

She received a dual Bachelor of Arts Degree in Communications and Social Sciences from the University of Southern California (USC) and later, a Master's Degree in Professional Writing, also from USC.

Mia lectures throughout Southern California on the development of screenplays, novels, and the creative process.

Stay in touch with Mia…

https://www.miawalshaw.com/
https://www.evatopia.com/

www.ingramcontent.com/pod-product-compliance
Lightning Source LLC
LaVergne TN
LVHW051554080426
835510LV00020B/2975